D1712017

Contents

Foreword

February 2017 opened a new chapter for Christian education around the world as eight different Christian school associations came together to encourage, support, and learn from one another, as well as celebrate the common bond of faith that inspires the life-saving work of sharing the gospel to the four corners of the globe. It was an unprecedented opportunity as these eight associations worked tirelessly for months to provide a platform to engage in conversation about the importance of working together and unifying around the core values that make Christian schools distinct. The 2017 Global Christian School Leadership Summit (GCSLS) was groundbreaking on so many different levels, but none more important than the opportunity that it provided for Christian educators, from so many different areas across the United States and around the world, to bring glory to God for His faithfulness.

World cultures are going through such rapid and profound change that Christians feel exiled in their own cities and towns. Christian schools are challenged with how to be salt and light in this new world without being of the world. I believe that is why God inspired Dan Egeler, president of the Association of Christian Schools International, to begin "a movement." He called on these eight different Christian school organizations "to lay down their individual flags and come together" in Orlando, Florida, in February 2017 to start a dialogue about the future of Christian education. Individuals from around the world responded in dramatic fashion, as over 700 people representing more than 250 schools from six continents came to celebrate the work that God is doing in and through Christian schools. The presence of the Holy Spirit was felt in a mighty way. The purpose of this book is to capture the spirit and dialogue of that gathering in order to create a sustainable and powerful movement.

I believe this movement is vitally important for many reasons, but I wish to highlight three. First, science, technology and engineering are advancing at such a rapid rate that they now have the capability of bringing unprecedented levels of prosperity to the world's poor, or alternatively they can literally destroy the world. Educating students in these areas in the context of the Christian worldview has never been more important. We need to work together to educate a generation of brilliant Christian engineers, scientists, and technologists who will view their careers as a sacred calling in the same way Christian pastors and teachers view their calling. We need to establish excellence in these areas that extend all the way through our Christian schools to our Christian universities; our Christian universities, in turn, need to stay faithful to their Christian missions.

Second, we need to work together to identify new financial models that will make Christian schools affordable to all socioeconomic classes of people around the world. In developed countries, Christian schools in many areas—but especially urban areas—are having a hard time staying financially sustainable. Strong Christian schools are one key to addressing the economic and moral challenges facing cities. The reason we made the decision to grow Grand Canyon University in an inner city is that we wanted it to serve as a model for how Christian schools can partner with urban community members to catalyze inner-city transformation. Christian schools should not shy away from working with municipalities, politicians, and social service agencies to help bring about transformative change to a community.

Third, we need to work together to identify models that successfully engage a rapidly changing culture. Jesus has called us to a radically different life. He highlighted the difference in the Sermon on the Mount when He said, "You have heard that it was said, 'Love your neighbor and hate your enemy. But I tell you, love your enemies and pray for those who persecute you'" (Matthew 5:43–44). The world marveled at the Christians in the first three centuries because they not only cared for their poor, but they also cared for those who oppressed them. Caring for people in need whether they agree with us or not is a powerful and winsome way to preach the gospel. I have found this generation of Christian young people very attracted to doing the work of the church in this way.

I am grateful to Dan Egeler for being inspired to bring us together as one body to start this movement of unity, and of reenvisioning Christian education for "such a time as this" (Esther 4:14). I am honored to be included and very excited to be part of its growth. Whether you attended the first summit or missed it, I highly encourage you to read this book, become part of the dialogue, and make plans to attend the next Global Christian School Leadership Summit.

Brian Mueller
President, Grand Canyon University
Phoenix, Arizona

Introduction

Stephen G. Reel and Lynn E. Swaner

"My goal is that they may be encouraged in heart and united in love, so that they may have the full riches of complete understanding, in order that they may know the mystery of God, namely, Christ, in whom are hidden all the treasures of wisdom and knowledge" (Colossians 2:2–3).

Paul's goal for believers, as expressed in his letter to the Colossian church, remains relevant for the body of Christ nearly two millennia later. In the face of increasing global interconnectedness, rapid technological change, and tectonic cultural shifts, Christians across the world are in great need of encouragement and unity, and the wisdom and knowledge found only in Christ. As Klaus Schwab observes in *The Fourth Industrial Revolution*, today's "changes are so profound that, from the perspective of human history, there has never been a time of greater promise or potential peril."[1] The church cannot adequately respond to this historical moment apart from a Colossians 2 experience. This is all the more true for Christian educators, who carry the awesome responsibility of preparing the next generation of gospel-bearers, culture-shapers, and world-changers.

It is most appropriate, therefore, that this passage of Scripture provided the banner for the inaugural Global Christian School Leadership Summit (GCSLS) in February 2017 in Orlando, Florida. The event was monumental in its size and scope (with over 700 Christian educators from 23 countries in attendance), as well as in its extraordinary display of unity (as the culmination of a shared vision by eight Christian school associations and five Christian universities).[2] The summit's purpose – to address current challenges in Christian education, identify strategic opportunities, and generate a collective vision for the future – was facilitated through collaborative engagement and sustained dialogue, held over three days and across 65 sessions. The words of one participant echo the sentiment we heard expressed by many:

"This has been one of the best experiences of my career in Christian education. Meeting and talking with like-minded colleagues from around the world has been most inspiring, informative, and unifying. The world today demands that Christian schools and leaders come together to tackle the very daunting tasks that lie ahead."

As an event that brought Christian school leaders together for this purpose, GCSLS was nothing short of unprecedented.

The potential for GCSLS's impact on kingdom education became evident months prior, as diverse organizations—many of which had no history of collaboration or even interaction—linked arms to sponsor and steer the event, and attendance grew by the hundreds. Along with this growth in unity and numbers, those responsible for planning increasingly realized that GCSLS could yield valuable insights and critical questions for the Christian education movement. If properly stewarded, this knowledge might well inform the direction of the movement into the next decade. This birthed a tremendous sense of responsibility and a corresponding strategy to capture the dialogue and emerging themes at the summit, which was accomplished through real-time data collection—mediated by mobile technology—of participants' reflections, personal applications, and questions. But by itself, this effort would not be enough. There had to be a means to further the critical conversations begun at GCSLS, both beyond the timeframe of the event, and beyond those in attendance. The book you now hold in your hands is precisely that.

The collective vision for this project was to craft a "centerpiece for continued dialogue" for both those who attended GCSLS and the broader Christian education community. To do this, the book asks three critical questions—as posed by Donovan Graham in *Teaching Redemptively*[3]—of the learning at the summit:

1. *What?* What was discussed at the summit, and what themes, ideas, and questions rose to the top as most important?

2. *So what?* Why do these themes, ideas, and questions matter to Christian education and to Christian educators?

3. *Now what?* Now that these themes, ideas, and questions have been identified, where do we go from here? What further work remains to be done?

In order to answer these questions, a group of leaders and thinkers in the Christian school movement assembled to serve as authors. Although recognized as subject matter experts, they did not write from that perspective. Rather, they assumed the role of "participant observers" who wrote from their collective insights from attending the summit, including participating in multiple sessions as well as the four plenaries (featuring Dan Egeler of ACSI; Lee Strobel, author of *The Case for Christ*; David Kinnaman of The Barna Group; and William Brown of The Colson Center for Christian Worldview), dialoguing with other attendees, reviewing the extensive participant feedback (collected through on-site research), and in some cases facilitating sessions themselves.

In synthesizing these various sources, the authors have crafted seven chapters; each chapter presents a major theme from the summit and encapsulates the best thinking and remaining questions surrounding theme.

- **Chapter 1, Sustainability for Christian Schools: Developing Spiritual and Operational Vitality.** Gene Frost (Wheaton Academy) and Glen Schultz (author of *Kingdom Education*) lay out the challenges to sustainability facing Christian schools, as well as how schools can focus on excellence while maintaining their mission in order to meet those challenges.

- **Chapter 2, Making Sense of Culture for the Christ-Centered School.** Bill Brown (The Colson Center for Worldview Development), Joel Gaines (Delaware County Christian School), and Dhugie Adams (Axis) discuss how to prepare Christian school students for engaging the cultural moment in general, as well as with the specific areas of diversity, LGBTQ issues, and technology.

- **Chapter 3, Engaged Learning: Building Capacity for 21st-Century Christian Education.** Lynn Swaner (ACSI) and Beth Ackerman (Liberty University) describe what it means to engage the 21st-century student in deeper learning, and how Christian school educators will need to develop both the mindset and skillset for doing so.

- **Chapter 4, Intersections of Faith and Science in Christian Education: Origins as an Opportunity.** Barrett Mosbacker (Westminster Christian Academy) and Jan Stump (The Colossian Forum) look at the relationship of faith and science in the Christian school, not as a battleground of ideology but as an opportunity to help students develop critical worldview-thinking skills, engage in informed and civil dialogue, and prepare to serve Christ in college and career.

- **Chapter 5, Relevance and the Christian School Movement: A Global Perspective.** Gavin Brettenny and Dan Egeler (both of ACSI) highlight trends impacting Christian education around the world, and share global perspectives on these trends—both as evidenced at GCSLS and from their experiences as leaders in a global Christian school association.

- **Chapter 6, Governing and Leading the Christian School: A Community-Based Approach.** Paul Campey (Resolve Consulting Group) and James Drexler (Covenant College) look at new and promising paradigms for governing and leading Christian schools that are more responsive to the challenges facing Christian education and faithful to biblical principles.

- **Chapter 7, Religious Liberties and a Faithful Christian Presence: Responding to Legal and Legislative Issues in Christian Education.** Mark Spencer (Christian Schools Australia) and Philip Scott (ACSI) consider how Christian schools across the globe can move from viewing legal and legislative issues solely in terms of self-preservation to engaging their broader societies through ambassadorship and advocacy.

At the end of each of these chapters the reader will find a set of discussion questions. We encourage you to gather others for conversation around these questions. After all, conversations are better when they involve others! We believe doing so will be fruitful and encouraging, whether you are a Christian school leader seeking to foster dialogue among teachers and staff, a higher education faculty member preparing future Christian school educators, a researcher considering potential areas for future inquiry, or a leader in Christian education who is strategizing for the future of the movement.

No matter how you came to this book or what role you play in Christian education, we urge you to carry the conversation forward. As one GCSLS participant wrote, "The potential for collaborative and supportive help… is tremendous. We are on the same journey, but with new friends. We need to walk together into the future, just as many walked together to make this event a reality." We invite you to walk with us.

Discussion Questions

1. How did this book make its way into your hands, and how is it appealing to you?

2. As you read this book, how can you draw others into the conversation alongside you?

3. What do you most hope to gain from this book?

NOTES

1 Klaus Schwab, *The Fourth Industrial Revolution* (New York: Crown Business, 2017), 2.

2 The eight partner associations for GCSLS were the Association of Christian Schools International (ACSI), Association of Christian Teachers and Schools (ACTS), the Council on Educational Standards and Accountability (CESA), Christian Schools International (CSI), the International Christian Accrediting Association (ICAA), the National Christian School Association (NCSA), Christian Schools Australia (CSA), and the Southern Baptist Association of Christian Schools (SBACS). In addition, Cairn University, Cedarville University, Columbia International University, Grand Canyon University, Liberty University, and The Colson Center for Christian Worldview cosponsored the event.

3 Donovan L. Graham, *Teaching Redemptively: Bringing Grace and Truth into Your Classroom* (Colorado Springs, CO: Purposeful Design Publications, 2nd ed.), xviii.

Chapter 1

Sustainability for Christian Schools: Developing Spiritual and Operational Vitality

Gene Frost and Glen Schultz

The dictionary definition of *sustain* includes: to keep in existence; to supply with necessities or nourishment; to support the spirits or resolution of; to endure or withstand; and to affirm the validity of.[1] Reading these definitions, it is evident that GCSLS itself was an exercise in promoting the sustainability of Christian schooling. Each chapter of this book relates to one or more of the above definitions.

Everything that schools do better, everything they appropriately add to their curriculum or program, every obstacle they overcome, and the degree to which Christian educators know and follow God's guidance all contribute to schools' sustainability. Thus, it is imperative that schools develop a strategy for addressing each of the various chapter topics and themes. Whether it is rigorous ongoing professional development that leads to engaged learning, or the legal and legislative challenges schools will face, each chapter highlights a major area schools need to consider. In fact, each chapter can serve as a kind of checklist to address as schools seek long-term sustainability.

The purpose of this chapter, however, is to frame the larger conversation of what it means to build sustainability across the Christian school movement. This chapter seeks to engage Christian educators in a conversation around sustainability by posing and addressing a number of questions, such as, What are current challenges to the sustainability of Christian schools? What is a biblical view of sustainability? How can Christian schools develop spiritual vitality as well as operational vitality, both of which are crucial for sustainability? What are some promising and best practices for Christian schools to address the challenges they currently face?

Challenges to Sustainability

Much of the conversation at GCSLS centered on new realities that Christian schools must take into account if they are seeking to be viable and relevant in today's culture. Key to this was a realization that Christians in Western countries no longer live in a cultural "Jerusalem" where there is a Judeo-Christian cultural consensus, but rather a cultural "Babylon." Unfortunately, many Christian schools continue to operate their schools as if the former were still the case.

One of the consequences of this is that Christian schools have not adjusted their marketing or their programs to attract the 21st-century customer, who has been influenced by living in Babylon. While the research shows that existing families with students in Christian schools place a high degree of value on aspects of those schools' Christian mission, mission-appropriate families who decide not to send their children to Christian schools place a greater emphasis on developing leadership and life skills. Christian schools, by and large, have not adjusted to provide opportunities for students to develop these skills, and therefore cannot market these opportunities to prospective families.

This shift reflects a dramatic change from the generation that founded Christian schools to the customers of today. Founding parents were largely loyal to their denominational and faith-based schools primarily because they were loyal to the idea of Christian schooling. This is why Catholics, Lutherans, and evangelicals filled their schools in the 60s and 70s. It was a truism that children certainly didn't tell their parents if they got paddled at school, because it would be worse when they got home. Students, families, and school leaders can't imagine thinking in these terms today.

Rather, today's families are no longer loyal to Christian education as a concept, and are far more concerned about the value of Christian schooling—not only in terms of its cost, but also in terms of the return on investment. Meeting the needs of each individual child, providing an academic and career "edge," and delivering a top-quality educational experience are the values sought by a new generation of families. Most school leaders can attest to this when they consider the characteristics of their school parents today. Attracting and retaining millennial parents is a distinct challenge, and running schools that fail to take into account and adjust to this reality will result in those schools becoming unsustainable.

Beyond these economic realities, there are other issues that arise from the current cultural moment. This includes political realities, such as the need to have policies in place to protect schools from lawsuits and adverse publicity (e.g., for their views on same-sex marriage or gender identity), and the real possibility that schools may eventually lose their tax-exempt status in the U.S. Again in the U.S., changing immigration policies may adversely impact international student programs. These and many other realities all directly affect a school's sustainability.

The Sustainer in Times of Challenge: A Biblical Reminder

In thinking about these challenges, it is important—before developing specific strategies to address them—to first provide a biblical view of sustainability through which to frame these challenges and solutions. Scripture provides historical records of leaders who saw God's sustaining hand as they focused on achieving God's mission for His people. These biblical accounts contain clear parallels with the experiences of many Christian schools with regard to sustainability. For example, Joshua and Caleb trusted in God and acted in faith on His promises when considering the very real challenges facing the Israelites in taking the Promised Land (fortified cities, well-trained and equipped armies, and giants). As a result, they—and none of the other ten spies who accompanied them on their reconnaissance trip—were the only two people out of an entire generation of Israelites who carried out God's mission to take possession of the land. They recognized that God had sustained them through the wilderness experience, and they believed He would continue to sustain them as they carried out His mission.

Recalling the comparisons drawn at GCSLS between the captivity in Babylon and the current cultural moment in which the church finds itself, the account of Ezra is particularly instructive. As an exile, Ezra was faced with seemingly insurmountable threats to the mission God had given him, but God used a pagan king to provide him with all of the funds, resources, and protection he needed to achieve that mission. The secret to Ezra's success was that "the good hand of his God was upon him. For Ezra had set his heart to study the law of the Lord, and to practice it, and to teach His statutes and ordinances in Israel" (Ezra 7:9–10, NASB). The reason Ezra experienced God's sustaining provision was because he had purposed in his heart to study God's Word, obey God's Word, and teach truth to all the people. This pattern of living is instructive today for Christian educators and school leaders in their mission to provide a Christian education in the midst of today's Babylonian culture.

Finally, chapter 14 of the Gospel of Matthew provides a very familiar picture of God's sustaining hand in the midst of storms. When Jesus came walking on the water toward the disciples' boat—which was stuck in the midst of a fierce storm and in danger of sinking— Peter stepped out of the boat and walked on the water toward the Master. It must be noted that when Peter got out of the boat, the sea was not calm. God did not still the waters and then call Peter to come to Him. The storm and the threat presented by the rough waters were still very real. However, when Peter kept his focus on Christ, he actually walked on the water toward the Lord. It was only when he started focusing on the threat of the rough seas around him that he was overcome and began to sink. When he came to his senses and called out to Christ to save him, the Lord brought him back to the safety of the boat. The lesson here is for Christian educators to remain focused on the Lord and His mission for their schools, even when they are walking on rough seas.

These scriptural examples should be a reassurance, regardless of the challenges to sustainability now facing Christian education. From these, it is clear that Christian educators can go to God—in whom is hidden the treasures of true wisdom and knowledge (Colossians 2:3)—as the Sustainer and the One who will enable Christian schools to survive both present and future challenges. With this encouragement in mind, this chapter turns now to examine two elements that are critical to the sustainability of Christian education: spiritual vitality and operational vitality.

Sustainability as Spiritual Vitality

At the foundation of Christian schools' efforts to provide a quality education for students is God's purpose and plan for education. If God's mission for Christian schooling does not remain the priority focus of Christian school leaders, mission drift will be a real threat and sustainability will become an impossibility. Christian schools must be grounded in and through spiritual vitality if they are to be sustainable. Four keys to spiritual vitality for Christian schools are the following:

Key #1. In order for Christian schooling to be sustainable, the home, church, and school must be united under a common cause. It is imperative that parents, pastors, church leaders, and educators be willing to address the issue of education biblically. Josh McDowell said it well in his foreword to *Kingdom Education: God's Plan for Educating Future Generations*: "The ideal way to help our kids not only to reject the postmodern worldview but also embrace deepened Christian convictions is to align church, home, and school into a unified whole that arms our children with the truth and protects them from distortions."[2]

Key #2. Christian parents, pastors, church leaders, and educators must continually strive to develop a strong biblical worldview in their own lives. Studies show that today's Christians may be the most biblically illiterate generation of believers in church history, and that a very small percentage of Christians possess a biblical worldview. Christians must be intentional in developing their own worldviews so that they interpret all of life from a solid biblical perspective. As parents, pastors, church leaders, and educators develop a biblical worldview, they will understand and be able to formulate a biblical philosophy of education that will lead them in engaging their families in Christian education.

Key #3. Christians must reject dualism, whereby they live their "religious" lives by biblical truth but their "secular" lives by human reasoning and common sense. This dualistic mindset has led the majority of Christians to see academic subjects as merely bodies of neutral facts with no spiritual meaning and, therefore, to not see the need for Christian education. Further, it results in their children considering God to be irrelevant to some areas of their lives. The reality is that Romans 1:20, Psalm 19:1–4, and other Scriptures make it clear that all of creation is an expression of who God is. Every subject taught, whether it is at home, church, or school, is part of His creation, and the study of these subjects is supposed to lead students to a deeper understanding of God's awesome nature in order to bring Him glory. All Christians, including those working in Christian schools, must be equipped to bring God-intended meaning back into the entire educational process.

Key #4. All Christians must pursue excellence in who they are and what they do, as they serve a God who is excellent (Psalm 8:1) and who expects His children to strive for excellence (Philippians 1). However, biblical excellence is vastly different from worldly excellence, which is based on horizontal comparison and competition with others (and as a result, often devalues character). By way of contrast, biblical excellence has a vertical perspective, where God is the standard, Jesus Christ is the model, the goal is Christlikeness, the focus is character, the basis is God's Word, and the motive is God's glory. (In this model of excellence, performance is an outgrowth of godly character.) When parents, church leaders, and educators understand and pursue biblical excellence, their educational efforts will be distinctive and stand apart from all other forms of schooling.

If parents, pastors, church leaders, and educators strive to put these keys into practice in their homes, churches, and schools, along with the resulting commitment to run an excellent school, Christian schooling will be spiritually vibrant and better positioned to survive contemporary and future challenges to sustainability.

Sustainability as Operational Vitality

In addition to spiritual vitality, Christian schools must be great, well-run educational institutions. Operational vitality must accompany spiritual vitality. The ACSI Formative to Flourishing Framework[3] provides a comprehensive picture of what operational excellence looks like in a Christian school. This school improvement model depicts schools as progressing along a continuum comprising four levels: formative, maturing, effective, and flourishing. As schools move along the continuum from formative to flourishing, they do so across six domains: board governance, executive leadership, school viability; student learning, spiritual formation, and school culture. It is imperative that Christian schools move quickly and effectively from formative to flourishing in order to ensure their sustainability in the 21st century.

One of the most effective ways to move from formative to flourishing is by the successful implementation of best practices. Best practices earn that title as the result of data that prove their effectiveness. Schools implement best practices when they make data-driven decisions, as opposed to decisions based on intuition, history, or aspiration. Unfortunately, Christian schools are not known on the whole for making data-driven decisions. In order to move toward this model of decision making, leaders must learn how to collect and analyze data in effective ways, how to conduct gap analyses (between how the school is performing and where it ought to be) based on that data, and how to prioritize and design strategies to address gaps. Many schools begin the journey to implementing best practices by gathering data through surveys. Student surveys, parent satisfaction surveys, and faculty and staff surveys can be used to help pinpoint the school's strengths and weaknesses. Surveys can be followed by qualitative measures, such as interviews and focus groups, to further explore the gaps in the school's mission attainment. This data can be used to identify and then implement the best practices that will address the issues raised.

On the leadership side, the management of Christian schools must change and adapt, particularly by adopting team-based approaches to leadership. Organizations that are led well by teams are more nimble and able to adapt creatively to challenges. This doesn't necessarily mean that the organizational hierarchy within a school must change, but rather that the way school leaders interact with others in the organization takes on a more team-like approach. A beginning point here can once again be data collection. Many school boards do a confidential 360-degree evaluation for the head of school every year, which asks teachers and staff to participate in the evaluation. Not only are valuable insights gained on the leadership style and team-building abilities of the head of school, but it also models to all the school's employees the willingness to be open to feedback. Finally, as many school leaders approach the age of retirement, succession plans need to be put into place for the next generation of Christian school leadership. This is essential to ensuring the sustainability of individual Christian schools as well as the Christian school movement as a whole.

In terms of financial management, fundraising and compensation models also must change in order to meet current challenges to sustainability. Fundraising and compensation are two different ends of the financial pipeline that both need attention, and for which Christian schools must identify and employ best practices. Fundraising helps to meet the financial needs of schools, and faculty and staff compensation is the largest expense at most schools. In terms of the latter, the question is whether a compensation model that promotes organizational effectiveness is in place at our schools; the traditional step scale model used by the public school is fatally flawed, and nothing like it is used for similar professional personnel in the business world. Christian schools must look for other compensation models to meet the needs of sustainability in the 21st century.

Program development and alternative revenue streams are also critical for operational vitality in the current environment. Whether international student programs, online or hybrid models, or excellent preschool programs, schools need to look beyond the traditional model for ways to expand their reach both in terms of mission and viability. Again, best practices should be sought and implemented when pursuing these opportunities. Finally, and along these lines, Christian schools may also need to explore new partnerships, since surviving on one's own is close to impossible in a cultural Babylon. At GCSLS, several presenters advocated for the need for Christian grade schools, high schools, colleges, universities, and ministries to work together in the greater enterprise of Christian schooling and education. These partnerships will make Christian education institutions "stronger together" in meeting the new realities of the 21st century.

There is no question that Christian school leaders and educators will be facing seemingly insurmountable challenges as they maneuver in a cultural Babylon. Sustainability in the face of these challenges, however, depends upon the response of schools and leaders. This response must be one of full reliance on God to provide all they need, and a firm commitment to developing and maintaining spiritual and operational vitality in Christian education.

Discussion Questions

1. What do you believe are the greatest threats to Christian school sustainability in the years ahead?

2. What are the top three challenges to your own school's sustainability?

3. What are you doing or what do you need to do to answer those threats and challenges?

4. How will you ensure that your school doesn't suffer from mission drift as you address the challenges of the 21st century?

NOTES

1 *The American Heritage Dictionary, Fourth Edition*, 2001, Houghton Mifflin Company.

2 Josh McDowell, "Foreword," in *Kingdom Education: God's Plan for Educating Future Generations*, Glen Schultz (Nashville, TN: LifeWay Press, 1998), 7.

3 Stephen P. Dill, "Moving from Formative to Flourishing," *Christian School Education*, 19 (1): 6-8.

Chapter 2

Making Sense of Culture for the Christ-Centered School

William E. Brown, Joel R. Gaines, and Dhugie Adams

From Augustine's *City of God*[1] to Richard Niebuhr's *Christ and Culture*,[2] scholarly works exploring the relationship of Christianity and the world around us have provided a wide array of theological and philosophical possibilities. Contemporary writers Andy Crouch,[3] James Davidson Hunter,[4] Rod Dreher,[5] Makoto Fujimura,[6] and others are giving carefully reasoned—and conflicting—approaches to living in this cultural moment. Christians are asked to consider any number of "options" for confronting our tech-saturated, sexuality-soaked culture. Since values and communication modes reboot about every five years, educators feel they are constantly twisting in societal winds.

The public views on issues ranging from sexuality and sexual identity to doctor-assisted suicide and embryonic stem cell research are shifting rapidly. Older conflicts focusing on race and gender are taking center stage again. The pages are turning quicker, and Christ-centered schools are finding it impossible to keep up with substantive cultural issues, let alone the constant flood of microtopics overwhelming their students.

Beyond the moral issues, the smothering presence of technology is redefining how we experience the world and interact with people in constantly new ways. For example, the always-insightful Axis Culture Insider recently warned, "Technology continues to shape us, especially children, more and more by way of new digital assistants. As these devices continue to proliferate, they shape the way children view social interactions and blur the lines on how we should interact with real people."[7]

No single path is obvious for Christ-centered schools to guide and equip students and their families in this confusing matrix. But one thing is certain: they cannot keep silent and take no notice of culture's influence.

Fulfilling the Mission

Christ-centered schools have a threefold mission: (1) providing students with a quality education, (2) informing and nurturing their faith, and (3) equipping them to biblically interact with the prevailing culture. The last of these is the most difficult. Following Christ means to lay bare one's sin and open oneself up for deeper friendships and accountability. To effectively navigate culture, the Christ-centered school must intentionally promote a constant public dialogue about issues of faith and culture. The days are gone when Bible classes and chapel can adequately equip students and families to maintain their faith and substantively interact with the culture.

Sometimes, the Christ-centered school finds itself in a position of uncertainty when it comes to engaging societal issues. By sending their children to a school, parents cede some responsibility for their education, often without knowing the school's approach to cultural engagement. Some parents may support a school's head-on encounters with issues as long as they are age-appropriate and biblical. Other parents may want to have these conversations with their own children. The partnership between the Christ-centered school and parents must become intentionally proactive and collaborative. Clearly, Christians cannot ignore the cultural challenges raised against the values and teachings of the family and school. The culture is speaking to children about these issues. Parents and Christian leaders should be there first, speaking competently and compassionately about the points of contact and conflict and equipping their students to respond in Christ-honoring ways.

Basic Commitments for the Christ-Centered School

As a foundation for developing a healthy approach to cultural engagement, here are four suggestions for the Christ-centered school:

1. The Christ-centered school must **develop an environment of cultural engagement**. While busy administrators and teachers have little discretionary time to study culture, the school can appoint a faculty or staff member to serve as a culture liaison to curate and disseminate the latest cultural topics to the school family. Several ministries, such as the aforementioned Culture Insider from Axis (ww.axis.org), provide regular cultural analysis. By providing awareness, understanding, and discernment, the school can model Christlike thinking and living to the school community. This may, in fact, be the most important practical equipping the school provides.

2. The Christ-centered school must **get parents informed and involved**. The opportunity to equip and disciple whole families is unique to the school. The mutual reinforcement helps provide a more consistent learning and living environment for the student. Required special meetings, webinars, and other programs can provide important insights to busy and disconnected families.

3. The Christ-centered school must **prioritize the development of substantive friendships among students**. Students encouraging and challenging one another can be the most effective influences on how they think and choose to live. When students care about each other's spiritual growth and share mutual accountability, many of the horizontal social distractions to learning recede. A school may supplement its chapel or discipleship program to provide time and space for the development of these relationships.

4. The Christ-centered school must **provide opportunities for students to dialogue, ask questions, and express doubts in a safe environment**. When students think they cannot express concerns and doubts about what is going on around them and within them, they may conclude that following Christ is irrelevant in the real world. Many interviews with former students who are no longer following Christ indicated the "close-minded" environment of their school as a factor in their life choice.

School leaders and teachers can model both openness and confidence in the faith even when they don't immediately have "all the answers." It is good for students to see mature examples of "the Lord's bondservant must not be quarrelsome, but must be kind to everyone" and "let your conversation be always full of grace, seasoned with salt, so that you may know how to answer everyone" (2 Timothy 2:24; Colossians 4:6, NIV).

Responses to Diversity, LGBTQ Issues, and Technology

The question is no longer *if* the Christ-centered school should interact with the prevailing culture but *how*. Doing so with an informed, biblical, and graceful approach models the mature Christians that schools hope their students will become. This chapter looks at three different cultural realities impacting students that emerged at GCSLS as pressing. Educator Joel Gaines explores the challenges and blessings of intentional diversity in the Christ-centered school. Bill Brown gives practical suggestions for how schools can teach and mentor their faculty and students effectively to equip them to understand and talk about LGBTQ issues in a Christ-centered manner. And Dhugie Adams, social analyst for Axis, weighs in with sound insights on technology and the Christ-centered school.

Diversity and the Christian School

What are the three topics you should not talk about in mixed company? One set of answers is race, politics and religion. I would argue that as Christians—specifically because of the gospel—we have the competence not only to talk about these three topics but to show answers from God's perspective from the Scriptures and in our lives. The main thing that keeps us from talking about these "controversial topics" is fear. Fear of the unknown, fear of saying the wrong thing, and fear of being exposed as ignorant or uneducated often holds us back from growing as professionals and individuals. Creating spaces in schools where teachers and students can have courageous conversations is a healthy necessity in the school's work toward being culturally competent. Teachers can be empowered to ask questions, exchange differing perspectives, and even disagree with the purpose of learning from others' experiences and perspectives. Students can have the freedom to learn how to express themselves in ways that are meaningful, honest, and even painful, yet in a context where their words are heard, valued, and considered. At this kairotic moment, Christian schools have a unique opportunity to publicly display the power of the gospel through intentional pedagogy and fearless conversations.

Many questions arise when trying to address the topic of diversity within the world of academia. How do we empower teachers and students to effectively listen and talk about differences within our schools from a biblical perspective? How do we help our teachers and students navigate a world that is so divided on topics of race, ethnicity, and culture? How do we garner support and promote diversity initiatives? The key is to begin conversations in schools to address these questions.

One way is to start or continue moving teachers, faculty, parents, and students to cultural proficiency. The goal is to help schools reflect and celebrate diversity because we see it highlighted by God in the Scriptures (Revelation 7:9). But before starting the hard work of substantive conversations, everyone must agree to a set of nonnegotiables. Here are the nonnegotiables our school uses when talking about diversity. Schools can modify these to fit the context; however, the following norms provide clarity to those involved. They allow room for honesty, openness and even mistakes.

- First, everyone must stay engaged in the conversation, even when it gets difficult or uncomfortable (Ephesians 4:3). In our dialogue and judgments we need to show respect. How we communicate with one another matters (Matthew 7:12). The conclusions we come to should be charitable and gracious.

- The next nonnegotiable is to expect and accept lack of closure. We are not trying to solve all the issues in one conversation. It may require follow-up questions or conversations.

- The last nonnegotiable is to have an enduring commitment to one another (Matthew 22:39). Everyone must commit to the process of learning, listening, and loving one another.

Once these norms have been established, there are specific pedagogies that promote conversation. Our teachers participate in roundtable discussions within their specific departments, and invite students into their professional development time. During these times, students can share ways cultural connections and ethnicity contribute to and impact the teachers' instruction. Required reading lists, question references, and lesson objectives impact their learning process. Teachers can take the thoughts and experiences shared during these dialogues and analyze their curriculum maps for areas of improvement. Often during the discussions students communicate an appreciation for the intentionality teachers put into their lessons when addressing areas of ethnicity. Other academic student groups share podcasts, TED talks, sermons, articles, and blogs with the department heads to review. The teachers and students then discuss the topics together.

The questions for school leaders are clear: Do teachers include students in their professional learning community? How would this be beneficial to the overall culture of your school academically? Have your teachers reviewed their pedagogy from the diverse cultural perspectives of the students within your school?

Finally, budget decisions, hiring, and the school board all have critical roles to play. A budget isn't just a financial document but also a moral document. How we prioritize our budgetary items shows what we value. For diversity initiatives to be embraced by faculty, staff, parents, and students, money must be allocated for their success. The fact that money is designated for an initiative tells all involved that the institution recognizes the importance of what is being done.

Diversity hiring has become a cultural buzzword in our society today. However, the issue is not cultural relevance, but whether the faculty and staff of your school reflect the ethnic makeup of the student body. Do students see individuals who look like them within the staff, teachers, administration, or board? It is just as important to have diversity within schools for all students. For minority students, it provides affirmation and understanding; for students in the majority, it provides insight and challenges biases.

In terms of hiring, a question that is often posed by school leaders is, Where are the qualified teachers of color? The answer is another question: Where are you looking? To find specialty items in a supermarket you have to go to the specialty aisle or you have to ask people who are familiar with that item so they can point you in the right direction. You can talk with community leaders, pastors, parents, undergraduate education departments, and masters-degree institutions—all great places for expressing desired faculty needs. One word of caution: do not "do diversity" for diversity's sake. It is important that the individuals you hire are mission-appropriate and the right fit for your context.

Finally, the school board plays a vital role in most of our schools, and similar questions need to be asked of them. Does the board reflect the diverse perspectives or ethnic makeup of the students at the school? A proven asset for schools is that the boards have representation of the diverse people groups in their community.

Courageous conversations lead to authentic relationships. Much of the work described above is done in professional development settings. Carving out time within our professional learning communities enables us to interact with topics that may not naturally come up throughout the rhythms of the normal school day. It is also important to include parents into the conversations in which your institutions is engaged, and ask, What are ways your school allows for the diverse voices in the community to be heard? One of the most powerful gifts you can give a person is the gift of being heard. Courageous conversations are initially awkward but have the potential to deepen relationships within the faculty, the student body, and the entire community for the glory of God.

Our LGBTQ World: Equipping Faculty and Students to Respond

The current cultural moment is defined by a new set of moral and religious imperatives circling around sexual identity and practice. How do we teach and mentor our faculty and students effectively to equip them to understand and talk about LGBTQ issues in a Christ-centered manner? Further, how do we serve students who find themselves experiencing same-sex attraction? We need to take an honest look at how we can maintain biblical teaching with practical, Christ-centered initiatives.

There are four specific steps for the Christian school to take. First, the school must develop an environment of cultural engagement, parental involvement, and honest dialogue. The opening section of this chapter discussed this need more fully.

Second, the school must provide information. The broad cultural acceptance of homosexuality, gender identification, and same-sex marriage has occurred at a lightning pace. In June 2011, President Obama reiterated his long-standing position of nonsupport for same-sex marriage. Within four years the Supreme Court's Obergefell decision made it the law of the land. For today's student, there is no shortage of information about LGBTQ stories and discussions in social and popular media. In fact, in the wider culture, it is approached as a settled matter. Leaders can be confident that older students have read a great deal, thought much, and talked at length with friends about LGBTQ issues. How information is presented sets the tone for this and other cultural topics.

In the Scriptures, three Old Testament and three New Testament passages speak directly to the issue of homosexuality: Genesis 19:1–10; Leviticus 18:22; Leviticus 20:13; Romans 1:26–27; 1 Corinthians 6:9; and 1 Timothy 1:9–10. Christian educators and students should be familiar with these texts. Helpful resources are available for the Christian teacher to understand these passages in context. Preston Sprinkle's book, *People to Be Loved: Why Homosexuality Is Not Just an Issue*[8] explores these texts from all positions and gives a biblical, theological, and historical perspective on them. For younger students, excellent age-appropriate resources are available to help them learn to process what they will encounter as they grow. Teachers need to know that there are valuable resources out there for both them and their students.[9]

Third, the school must model a Christ-centered response. Because of the prevailing culture, most schools have students who are questioning their own sexual orientation. Almost all of them know someone who is. Schools should provide opportunities for discussion and mentoring. Use YouTube videos of speakers such as Wesley Hill, Christopher Yuan, and others who speak as followers of Christ who acknowledge same-sex attraction and their commitment to a Christ-centered life. Their approach is one of compassion and understanding, providing a powerful antidote to the unbiblical and shrill attacks from others.

Finally, the school must broaden its understanding of the relational future of its students. Emphasizing the importance of genuine friendships can lay the groundwork for personal and spiritual stability. For some, singleness will be the course of their lives. Churches and schools rarely acknowledge singleness as a valid option (Paul calls it a "gift" in 1 Corinthians 7:7) and do little to help those who choose to follow Christ in this way.

Navigating the Technology Superhighway

Consider this: you live in a small town with many local roads. They are adequate for a time, but the population has reached the point of needing a highway system. The local officials, wanting to "keep up," decide to build a network of highways to open up new ways of commuting. But instead of doing their due diligence to ensure the highways are designed to make travel more effective, they just start placing highways randomly. Would this solve the problem? Maybe you would solve some of the problems randomly, but not likely. What kinds of problems does building roads without planning create? Traffic jams, accidents, extended commute times? We can agree that placing highways randomly would be an irresponsible way to approach roadway planning.

And yet, have we taken this approach to technology in schools? Assuming we recognize the need for technology in our schools, we must start thinking about a "philosophy of technology." Knowing what questions to ask when implementing a technology program in our schools is crucial. The way we choose to engage with technology in our schools might differ from how our neighbor chooses to do so—and that's OK! Each school has its own unique needs and challenges to take into consideration.

Let's start off with the "philosophy of technology." Think of this as a school's mission statement for the use of technology, which should answer the following questions: Why are we using technology? What kind of technology do we need? How does it tie into the overall mission and vision of our school? While technology is a wonderful servant, it can be a terrible master. Technology is an effective tool that can aid in teaching and learning. But similar to the example of planning new roadways for a city, if we do not have a clear mission and vision for technology, it can—and most likely will—be used in inappropriate or counterproductive ways. Schools must determine where technology will be used to advance the overall mission and where it will not.

Once the school has determined its technology philosophy, there are a few cornerstone questions that should be asked about implementing technology. The questions will vary based on what technology is chosen for the school and how it will be used. As a starting point, the following questions should be asked. First, How will this technology empower our students to take control of their own learning? You might have noticed that more families have chosen to homeschool their students lately, and one of the primary reasons is the ability to customize a student's learning. By integrating new technologies, a school can offer students the ability to learn in new ways and broaden the school's curriculum with classes online that are not offered on campus.

The second question is, Who is responsible for providing the technology? These days, smartphones, tablets, and laptops are accessible to nearly every student. Determining whether the school or the student will supply the technology is important. There are challenges on both sides. If the school provides devices, there is a major cost, but the school retains the ability to monitor activity more easily. If the students provide the devices, the cost is removed from the school, but providing accountability can be a nightmare. Both are reasonable options, but the school must decide which works best.

This leads to the practical issue of dealing with technology distraction: how much personal technology will the school allow students to use—and when they can use it? Some schools require students to turn off (or turn in) their smartphones during the school day except for predesignated short periods of time. Others deal with the distraction issues in different ways. Whatever the policy, it must be clearly understood and enforced. Helping students understand the spiritual and social challenges of personal technology is an important part of their education. A good resource is Dr. Kathy Koch, who has written helpful books on teens and technology, most notably the excellent *Screens and Teens: Connecting with Our Kids in a Wireless World*.[10] Another is *The Tech-Wise Family: Everyday Steps for Putting Technology in Its Proper Place*,[11] by Andy Crouch, whose practical recommendations for families can be carried over into the school.

The third, and in some ways most important question, is this: Is the proper support in place for integrating technology? Before bringing in any new technology, such support needs to exist. Technology may fail, security may be breached, or unanticipated problems may arise. Adequate support must exist on the back end to address each scenario. This is both a personnel and a funding issue to be decided as the school develops its philosophy.

The most helpful suggestion is for each school to gather as much information as possible, particularly from other schools trying to optimize their use of technology and to guide their students to use it in a Christ-centered way. Sharing best practices and strategies will help students get the most from technology and overcome the challenges inherent in its constant presence. These commitments are critical for schools to equip students for living in this cultural moment for the glory of God.

Culture and the Christ-Centered School

Equipping students to flourish in the faith and draw others to Christ is a blessed challenge. It will not happen without an intentional "face the culture" milieu in the school and a positive attitude toward the opportunities to make a difference. Tackling the challenging areas of racial diversity, LGBTQ issues, and technology (and many more to come) with the heart and mind of Christ is essential if Christian educators are to model the life of the mind and heart they envision for their students.

Discussion Questions

1. Do our students feel comfortable asking questions and sharing their struggles and doubts with school leadership and faculty?

2. Do school leaders and teachers regularly engage with students about issues of race, sexual identity, etc.?

3. Are we intentionally modeling and teaching the biblical truth of sexuality, friendship, and singleness?

4. Is the presence of technology (from students' smartphones to the school's network) a value-added or a distraction on our campus—or both?

NOTES

1 Augustine, *The City of God* (English reprint version, New York: Random House, 1994).

2 H. Richard Niebuhr, *Christ and Culture* (New York: Harper & Row), 1951.

3 Andy Crouch, *Culture Making: Recovering Our Creative Calling* (Downers Grove, IL: IVP Books, 2008).

4 James Davison Hunter, *To Change the World: The Irony, Tragedy, and Possibility of Christianity in the Late Modern World* (Oxford: Oxford University Press, 2010).

5 Rod Dreher, *The Benedict Option: A Strategy for Christians in a Post-Christian Nation* (New York: Penguin, 2017).

6 Makoto Fujimura, *Culture Care: Reconnecting with Beauty for Our Common Life* (Downers Grove, IL: IVP Books, 2017).

7 Axis, www.axis.org, "The Culture Insider," vol. 3, Issue 10, March 10, 2017.

8 Preston Sprinkle, *People to Be Loved: Why Homosexuality Is Not Just an Issue* (Grand Rapids, MI: Zondervan, 2015)

9 Stan and Brenna Jones, *God's Design for Sex Series*, 4 Books (Carol Stream, IL: Navpress/Tyndale House Publishers. 2007); Justin Holcomb and Lindsey Holcomb, *God Made All of Me: A Book to Help Children Protect Their Bodies* (Greensboro, NC: New Growth Press, 2015); Kristen Jenson and Gail Poyner, *Good Pictures Bad Pictures: Porn-Proofing Today's Young Kids* (Richland WA: Glen Cove Press, 2014).

10 Kathy Koch, *Screens and Teens: Connecting with Our Kids in a Wireless World* (Chicago: Moody Press, 2015).

11 Andy Crouch, *The Tech-Wise Family: Everyday Steps for Putting Technology in Its Proper Place* (Grand Rapids, MI: Baker Books, 2017).

Chapter 3

Engaged Learning: Building Capacity for 21st-Century Christian Education

Lynn E. Swaner and Beth Ackerman

Whether developing students' biblical worldview, preparing graduates for higher education and vocational life, or inspiring students to Christlike service, the goals of Christian education's mission statements are inspirational. But to what degree are they aspirational? In other words, do schools and institutions really achieve all of the desired student outcomes—including spiritual, academic, behavioral, and social—that populate their mission statements?

The 2014 Cardus Education Survey provides insightful data on this question. In terms of spiritual outcomes, the survey found that graduates of evangelical Protestant schools outpaced their peers from all other types of schools (public, nonreligious private, or Catholic) in their giving to religious organizations, attending religious services, seeking jobs that fulfill a religious calling, believing in the infallibility of the Bible, and praying at home.[1] Although these outcomes cannot be wholly attributed to Christian school attendance—as students' home and church experiences undoubtedly play a part—Christian schools clearly have a positive impact on students' spiritual development. As the Cardus report concludes, "The fact that Evangelical schools institutionalize the importance and practice of religiosity appears to have a longer-term impact on graduates."[2]

On many academic outcomes, however, graduates of evangelical Protestant schools were outpaced by those from other types of private schools, and were on par with their peers in public schools. This includes the number and level of higher math and science courses taken, total years of education obtained, and the likelihood of obtaining a graduate degree. And as compared with graduates from both public and all other private schools, Christian school graduates were less likely to pursue a STEM major in college, and the colleges and universities they attended were often less selective. This suggests that there is a disparity between the attainment of spiritual and academic outcomes at Christian schools—which ultimately can limit Christian school graduates' abilities to fulfill the Great Commission (Matthew 28:19–20) and the Creation Mandate (Genesis 1:28) through vocational and relational ministry across disciplines and contexts.

How to address this concern was a topic of significant discussion at the 2017 Global Christian School Leadership Summit (GCSLS). Teachers expressed dismay over widespread student disengagement in the classroom. School leaders wondered how to motivate faculty to focus on improving student outcomes. Board members worried about market-savvy parents seeking greater educational ROI for their tuition dollars.[3] University faculty grappled with how to prepare Christian school teachers for the realities of the 21st century. And across these groups, Christian educators expressed a deep desire to "excel still more" (1 Thessalonians 4:1, NASB) in attending to all of the facets of their mission statements, thereby preparing students to fulfill God's unique call on their lives.

As is typical for most complex problems in education, however, no single answer to these questions exists (and not surprisingly, one was not forthcoming at the summit). Yet while there may not be a panacea, there does appear to be promise—meaning that there are pedagogical and organizational approaches that emerged during the summit that have significant potential for impact. These promising approaches reflect, in the words of Sir Ken Robinson, "Not the old style of industrial education, which was designed to meet the needs of the nineteenth and early twentieth centuries, but a new style of education suited to the challenges we now face and the real talents" of today's students.[4] For the purpose of this chapter, we have gathered these approaches under one umbrella: "engaged learning."

Engaged learning is simultaneously two things: (1) a set of learner-centered pedagogies that attend to a range of student outcomes; and (2) a schoolwide cultural orientation, from which flow organizing principles for school life. As such, engaged learning requires significant shifts in "business as usual" at Christian schools, as well as the development of a different skillset—and as importantly, a different mindset—on the part of Christian educators. Drawing upon insights from GCSLS, this chapter will outline the case for engaged learning, frame a portrait of it in practice, and describe the necessary conditions for realigning Christian education toward student engagement.

The Case for Engaged Learning

When Christian educators at GCSLS were asked to describe today's learner, many responded with descriptors like "overwhelmed," "entitled," "unmotivated," and "distracted," with reasons for these traits including a collapse in family structure, the pervasive influence of technology, diverse learning needs and abilities, and the negative impact of a post-Christian society. This perspective of today's students, and the cultural moment in which they are situated, was framed in terms of a monumental challenge to the task of educators.

However, looking back on the perceptions of a generation or two ago—and examining outcome data for that generation—can provide encouragement. Back in 1999, when the last wave of Gen-Xers (panned as the "lost generation"[5]) was graduating college, Norman Furniss wrote an influential chapter on higher education entitled "Barbarians Inside the Gate?

Why Undergraduates Always Seem Worse and Civilization as We Know It at the Brink." Just the title alone makes a forceful point, but Furniss' description of a "widespread … feeling that college students today are disturbingly different from both their professors and previous generations of students"—who have "fundamentally distinct morals and values" and are "ignorant of and indifferent to the academic enterprise"[6]—sounds familiar nearly twenty years later. This fundamentally proves the title's thesis. And outcome data on Gen-Xers in the workplace suggests that they ended up well outpacing other generations—even Boomers—in terms of adaptability, problem solving, collaboration, and especially revenue generation[7] (recall that Gen-Xers led the tech boom).

Of course the jury is still out on today's generation of students, but there are a few lessons to be learned here. First, while there are differences in the learners of each generation, what seems to remain constant is the gap between learners and the adults who teach them—and it is the task of each generation of educators to find ways to bridge it. Second, Christian educators can find a more missional way to view student differences, by reframing them biblically: that is, in terms of God's unique design and preparation for today's students to serve "God's purpose" in their own generation, like David (Acts 13:36). This enables educators to focus on students' differences as strengths rather than deficits, which—when nurtured and pointed in the right direction—will prepare students to be culturally relevant ministers of the gospel and fruitful stewards of creation. By way of example, today's students can be viewed either as technologically distracted nomads who are addicted to their devices, or as digital natives who are poised to use cyberspace to bring the gospel to "the whole world as a testimony to all nations" and usher in the return of Christ (Matthew 24:14). The difference between these two futures may well depend on Christian educators' ability to bridge the gap between how they teach and how students learn.

By definition, engaged learning—or pedagogical approaches that deeply involve students in their learning, situated within an overall culture of student engagement—bridges that gap. In many ways, engaged learning is nothing new; educators have been talking about differentiated instruction, student-centered pedagogy, authentic assessment, and the like for years. The reality, however, is that engaged learning still runs countercultural to the dominant model of education in the U.S. that is based on a one-size-fits-all approach, conformity to standards tied to age and grade level, and standardized testing results as the ultimate gauge of student learning. The contrast is so stark that educational environments constructed around engaged learning are often labeled "alternative," which is the point made again by Sir Ken Robinson[8]:

> These are programs designed to get kids back into education. They have certain common features. They're very personalized. They have strong support for the teachers, close links with the community and a broad and diverse curriculum, and often programs which involve students outside school as well as inside school. And they work. What's interesting to me is, these are called "alternative

education" … [but] all the evidence from around the world is, if we all did that, there'd be no need for the alternative.

While this divide may extend to much of Christian education as well, judging from the dialogue at GCSLS, there is a groundswell of interest among Christian educators to rethink teaching and learning in terms of better engaging students. And increasingly, educators are perceiving the promise of engaged learning for achieving all of the diverse goals in their school mission statements.

A Portrait of Engaged Learning

As mentioned earlier, engaged learning is fundamentally: (1) a set of learner-centered pedagogies that attend to a diverse range of student outcomes; and (2) a schoolwide cultural orientation, from which flow organizing principles for school life. Not to be confused with humanistic philosophies of education, a Christian view of engaged learning is grounded in Scripture and congruent with a biblical worldview. For Christian educators, truth remains fixed in the Person of Jesus and the Word of God (John 14:16, John 17:17, 2 Timothy 3:16), authorities are to be respected (Hebrews 13:17), and honor is to be given to those to whom it is due (Romans 13:7). In the same passage of Scripture in which children are instructed to obey, however, parents (and by extension, educators) are told to not "exasperate your children; instead, bring them up in the training and instruction of the Lord" (Ephesians 6:1–4). What should such effective training and instruction look like?

Three relevant principles are found in Scripture. First, a Christian philosophy of engaged learning acknowledges that God has created students as whole beings (mind, body, soul, spirit) in His image (Genesis 1:27, Psalm 49:9). Christian education must therefore educate the whole person by attending to these domains. Second, God has made each person unique, "just as he wanted them to be" (1 Corinthians 12:17–20), and has endowed them with "different kinds of gifts … for the common good" (1 Corinthians 12:4–7). Christian education ought to celebrate this diversity through differentiated instruction and learner-centered teaching. And thirdly, Christian education should prepare students for the good works that God has intended for them to do (Ephesians 2:10, 2 Timothy 3:16–17), by providing opportunities for hands-on learning and skill building.

Taken together, these three principles can be seen reflected in Jesus' own approach to teaching, which included a range of instructional methods, including didactic teaching, narrative and storytelling (parables), modeling (washing the disciples' feet), guided practice (feeding of the 5,000), and unsupervised practice (sending the disciples out in pairs). Put simply, it will be "enough" for Christian educators to be like their own teacher, Jesus (Matthew 10:25). The task of Christian educators is to translate these principles into the 21st-century classroom (which, it should be noted, is itself an exercise in biblical integration).

When making this translation, it is helpful to think in terms of a set of "dimensions" to which the learning experience must attend if it is to engage students fully. These dimensions emerge from the literature and research on how students learn best, and which educational practices have significant impact on student outcomes.[9] Four such dimensions are:

1. *The holistic dimension*, by which the learning experience attends to multiple domains of learning (e.g., cognitive, affective, behavioral, spiritual)

2. *The developmental dimension*, which means that learning not only encompasses holistic domains, but also encourages growth and development toward complexity in those domains (e.g., in students' ways of thinking, feeling, acting, and believing)

3. *The contextual dimension*, which involves the social aspects of learning, by promoting students' interdependence and engagement in community

4. *The integrative dimension*, which entails helping students to integrate various sites, sources, modalities, and time periods of learning—often through active, hands-on learning combined with ongoing opportunity for reflection—thereby enabling students to "connect the dots" in their understanding and to see their education and life experiences as an integrated whole

This is certainly not an exhaustive list of ingredients, as it were, that combine to make a learning experience engaged. However, as Swaner (2012) explains, "educational settings that activate these dimensions not only facilitate gains in knowledge, real-world application of learning, and intellectual complexity, but also … facilitate the transformational experiences we might consider engaged learning."[10]

A wide range of instructional practices that harness these dimensions emerge from the literature and research, and also were discussed by GCSLS participants. It is helpful to group these various teaching approaches and pedagogies into two different levels (the classroom, and the school/institution), as well as into two tiers (which progress in terms of greater encompassment of the learning environment).[11] A sample of these practices is grouped by level and tier in the following table.

Level	Tier 1	Tier 2
Classroom	• Homework options • Varied journal prompts • Varied pacing • Student/teacher goal setting • Varied technology • Varying graphic organizers • Think-Pair-Share • Stations and centers • Choices of books and materials • Flipped classroom • Flexible seating	• Differentiated learning products • Labs • Independent studies • Learning contracts • Choice of assessment, including rubrics, portfolios • Hybrid learning (online, in-class) • Peer teaching and assessment • Circles (literature, interest) • Teams, games, tournaments • Flexible classroom setup
School/ Institutional	• Shared planning and/or collaboration time for teachers • Differentiated curricula or courses of study for students • Electives through online programs and colleges • J-term or winter-term • Mini-courses/electives • Community mentors • Shared learning spaces (for multiple classrooms/grades) • STEM/STEAM labs	• Coteaching • Capstone courses • Significant coursework or curriculum built around problem-based learning, action research, or service-learning • Internships/practica/co-op • Student/teacher learning communities • Community partnerships and exchanges • Flexible learning spaces throughout the school/institution

In presenting this as a portrait, it is important to understand that engaged learning is best conceptualized as an intentionally crafted landscape. Thus, this is not offered as a menu of choices that—taken together—would lead to student engagement, but rather as evidences of an overall instructional culture that values engaged learning and intentionally works to engage students through instructional practice.

Finally, it is important to note that integrating a biblical worldview is not specifically listed at either level or tier. This is because it is assumed that teaching in a Christian school means at least two things: (1) to teach the content from a biblical worldview, rooted and grounded in the truth of God's Word; and (2) to teach it by a process that is congruent with biblical principles of instruction (as outlined previously) and thereby engages students in their learning. Education from a biblical worldview thus necessarily involves both the content and the process of learning—and, arguably, must be engaged.

What Will It Take?

At this point, readers may share the sentiment of many GCSLS participants: "What will it take?" Participants repeatedly asked this question on feedback surveys for every session related to engaged learning. Specifically, they wondered what it would take for educators to transform their classrooms and schools, to inspire their teachers to change, to address all of the outcomes in their mission statements, and to even get started in the process.

The good news is that Christian schools have already begun experimenting with ways to build capacity for student engagement. Special J-term courses, hybrid classes that take advantage of online learning platforms, and block scheduling were early attempts at integrating engaged learning into the regular school year and day. These efforts seem to have made headway in Christian schools, and certainly are commendable (surely students' dashing from one 38-minute period to the next, nine times a day, is not conducive to student engagement). Having already instituted these approaches, some Christian schools are beginning to roll out next-level structural changes—for example, "blowing up" a full day of the school week, by halting the regular schedule for that day and filling it with special courses or experiences (e.g., student-selected electives, STEM lab classes, leadership courses, or internships).

While anecdotal reports from these schools suggest that such structural changes are promising, they do not always seem to correlate with changes in the ways teachers actually teach. (It may be that you can take teachers out of the traditional classroom, but you can't always take the traditional classroom out of teachers!) Structures that build capacity for engaged learning do just that—they build capacity—but that capacity still needs to be realized with pedagogies that elicit engagement. To this end, an even smaller number of Christian schools are exploring specific pedagogies for engaged learning (i.e., problem-based learning, action research, and service-learning). These pedagogies have been shown through research to boost a range of student outcomes[12], many of which are congruent with Christian schools' mission statements. They all emphasize process skills over content mastery, place more responsibility for learning on the student, require ongoing collaboration among students, transform the role of the teacher to more of a guide than an expert, and necessitate nonlinear and diverse assessments of learning (e.g., portfolios, usable products).

Successfully implementing these pedagogies across Christian education will require a fundamentally different mindset and skillset of educators. In terms of mindset (alternatively called a "disposition" in the literature), engaged learning requires teachers to view everyone in the school community as learners—including themselves. As Carol Dweck explains: "Fixed-mindset teachers often think of themselves as finished products. Their role is simply to impart their knowledge" whereas "great" teaching "starts with the growth mindset—about yourself and about children. Not just lip service to the idea that all children can learn, but a deep desire to reach in and ignite the mind of every child."[13] Having a growth mindset predisposes teachers to embracing the complexity, challenges, and joys of engaged learning, but having a fixed mindset will likely result in the exact opposite. This has profound implications for teacher educators as they instruct and supervise pre-service teachers, as well as for school leaders responsible for hiring new teachers and supervising current ones. At each point in a teacher's development—from pre-service to orientation to in-service—this mindset needs to be cultivated, reinforced, and rewarded if teachers are to value and practice engaged learning. And this same mindset is likewise needed by instructional leaders, who are responsible for creating school environments, systems, and ultimately cultures that support engaged learning.

A mindset conducive to engaged learning is, in fact, a precondition for developing the skillset for engaged learning. Engaged learning requires a blurring of the lines between "hard skills"—like content knowledge (e.g., chemistry or third-grade English language arts) and pedagogical knowledge (lesson planning, biblical integration, classroom management)—and "soft skills," like process-mindedness, creativity, teamwork, and flexibility. Engaged learning pedagogies require that these skills be blended to create learning environments that are highly collaborative, feedback rich, and process-as-content oriented. Likewise, instructional leaders need a special skillset for creating cultures of engagement in their schools, to include systems thinking, innovation, and change management.

Skill sets are developed through introduction to new skills (via instruction and modeling), ample opportunity for practice, and ongoing feedback from others. Arguably, the primary way that educators have opportunity to develop their skillsets is through in-service professional development (PD). And this is where GCSLS participants identified a major gap in their ability to implement engaged learning. A recent literature synthesis on best practices in Christian school PD (by one of this chapter's authors, and presented at GCSLS) found that, overall, there is room for improvement in terms of increasing PD duration and practicality for teachers, as well as incorporating more active learning and collaboration.[14] This is compounded by a lack of PD opportunities that intentionally support and promote engaged learning, for both teachers and instructional leaders. Developing systematic PD thus represents a significant challenge for Christian schools seeking to implement engaged learning.

The good news is that, as suggested by the findings of the literature synthesis, best practices in PD may themselves help to foster engaged learning:

> Some research suggests that the success of PD efforts is not dependent on the specific formulation of PD, but rather is directly linked to the presence of a schoolwide orientation toward continuous improvement. This view does not limit PD to a single practice or even a collection of practices, but rather views PD as part of a larger approach to reshape the underlying values of the school community.[15]

This re-envisioning no longer considers PD as something external in which educators participate, or that must be developed as an "add-on" to the school calendar. Rather, optimal

PD involves a whole-school transformation into a community of learners, who have time embedded for reflection, collaboration, experimentation, and feedback within the regular school day. This kind of learning community is well-suited for engaged learning, which itself shares many of the same features.

At its heart, Christian education involves intergenerational transfer, whereby teachers declare God's power "to the next generation" (Psalm 71:1) as well as prepare students to serve "God's purpose" in their own generation (Acts 13:36). At GCSLS, engaged learning emerged as a promising means for helping schools and institutions to do just that—and in doing so, fulfill their multifaceted mission statements. Further thinking, research, and discussion are needed around the ways schools and institutions can develop classrooms and cultures of engagement, thereby building capacity for 21st-century Christian education.

Discussion Questions

1. How can you go about conducting an audit (either informally or formally) of where your school or institution is successfully engaging students in learning?

2. What are some ways you can build capacity for engaged learning, so that more students are engaged for more of the time?

3. What challenges do you face in implementing engaged learning, at both the classroom and school/institution levels?

4. What resources or strategies might be needed to address those challenges?

NOTES

1 Ray Pennings et al., *Cardus Education Survey* (Hamilton, Ontario: Cardus, 2014).

2 Ibid., 28.

3 Academic ROI played heavily into discussions at GCSLS around sustainability. Put simply, demand for a product is usually directly related to its quality. One retired head of school at the summit shared her story of being hired to lead a struggling school. A few weeks into the job, her board chair asked when she was going to "get out there and start fundraising," to which she responded, "When we have an academic program that's worth raising funds for." She spent the next three years building a stellar academic program, and not long after the school grew into one of the most successful in the region—thanks to her insistence and persistence when it came to excellence in teaching and learning.

4 Ken Robinson and Lou Aronica, *Creative Schools: The Grassroots Revolution That's Transforming Education* (New York: Penguin Books, 2015), xxv–xxvi.

5 Joel Kotkin and Wendell Cox, "Generation X's Moment of Power Is Almost Here," *Forbes*, December 28, 2016, https://www.forbes.com/sites/joelkotkin/2016/12/28/generation-xs-moment-of-power-is-almost-here/#4227198f2d4b.

6 Norman Furniss, "Barbarians at the Gate? Why Undergraduates Always Seem Worse and Civilization as We Know It at the Brink," in *The Social Worlds of Higher Education: Handbook for Teaching in a New Century*, ed. Bernice A. Pescosolido and Ronald Aminzade (Thousand Oaks, CA: Pine Forge Press, 1999), 154.

7 Ernst & Young, "Younger managers rise in the ranks: survey quantifies management shift and reveals challenges, preferred workplace perks, and perceived generational strengths and weaknesses," news release, September 3, 2013.

8 Ken Robinson, "How to Escape Education's Death Valley" (TED talk, April 2013), 14:54-16:04.

9 Lynn Swaner, "The Theories, Contexts, and Multiple Pedagogies of Engaged Learning: What Succeeds, and Why?" in *Transforming Undergraduate Education: Theory that Compels and Practices that Succeed*, ed. Donald W. Harward (Lanham, MA: Rowman & Littlefield Publishers, Inc., 2012), 73–89.

10 Ibid., 75.

11 Adapted from Beth Ackerman, *G.U.I.D.E.: Differentiated Instruction for Christian Educators* (Lynchburg, VA: Liberty University Press), 10–11, and Lynn Swaner, "The Theories, Contexts, and Multiple Pedagogies of Engaged Learning: What Succeeds and Why?" in *Transforming Undergraduate Education: Theory that Compels and Practices that Succeed*, ed. Donald W. Harward (Lanham, MD: Rowman & Littlefield Publishers, Inc., 2012), 73–89.

12 Jayne Brownell and Lynn Swaner, *High-Impact Practices: Applying the Learning Outcomes Literature to the Development of Successful Campus Programs* (Washington, D.C.: Association of American Colleges and Universities, 2010).

13 Carol S. Dweck, *Mindset: The New Psychology of Success* (New York: Ballantine Books, 2016), 204–5.

14 Lynn Swaner, *Professional Development for Christian School Educators and Leaders: Frameworks and Best Practices* (Colorado Springs, CO: Association of Christian Schools International, 2016).

15 Ibid., 4.

Chapter 4

Intersections of Faith and Science in Christian Education: Origins as an Opportunity

Barrett Mosbacker and Jan Stump

"Houston, we have a problem" is a classic line from the movie *Apollo 13*. It has become popular shorthand for the emergence of any unforeseen problem. Like the one facing the crew of Apollo 13, we have a problem in our Christian schools that threatens our credibility and the future of our students. Our problem is that the intersections between faith and science in the Christian school are often viewed as a battleground of ideology to be avoided, rather than a rich opportunity to help students develop critical worldview thinking skills, engage in informed and civil dialogue, and prepare to serve Christ in college and career. Origins is a key intersection between faith and science, and an area of opportunity in which the Christian school can engage students in a rigorous and academically honest discussion, including how to square scientific evidence with an uncompromising commitment to God's infallible Word.

If origins are discussed in the classroom in a scientifically simplistic and theologically shallow manner, the result is disingenuous and dangerous for our students. Avoiding a robust, academically honest discussion of origins is dangerous for our students because they may encounter a crisis of faith when they enter university. They will not be prepared for the evidence, nuance, and complexities of the scientific disciplines presented by smart, articulate professors. This can create one of two responses by many Christian students. One, they can ignore the scientific evidence presented for evolution and simplistically convince themselves that it is simply not true. Two, those of a more intellectually curious and skeptical mind may face a crisis of faith brought about by a cognitive dissonance for which they have not been prepared.

To send our students unprepared into the university or into the workplace without a thorough understanding of scientific evidence for evolution, the complexities of biblical interpretation, and without a basic understanding of the symbiotic relationship between God's revelation through the written word and creation is antithetical to our mission of preparing our students to engage the world for Christ. Sadly, many of these students abandon their faith or banish it to the inner rooms of their personal spiritual lives where it has little influence on their professional work.

There is an understandable reason why the topic is avoided or only dealt with in a simplistic and "safe" manner: origins is a dangerous topic. For the Christian school, origins is what is often referred to as the "third rail." In politics, the third rail is a metaphor for any issue so controversial that it is "charged" and "untouchable" to the extent that any politician or public official who dares to broach the subject will invariably suffer—he or she is most likely to be politically electrocuted by opponents and the electorate. Social Security is such a political third rail. According to Henry Hubbard, former Washington correspondent for *Newsweek*, the phrase originates with Kirk O'Donnell, a top aide to Tip O'Neill. The full quote is: "Social Security is the third rail of American politics. Touch it, you're dead."[1]

No one desires to be shocked, let alone electrocuted! It is not surprising then that origins is not openly discussed in many Christian school classrooms. The topic of creation and evolution produces palpable fear. The fear is real and justified. Few topics engender such heated passion among evangelicals as to how to interpret the first chapters of Genesis and to square those interpretations with scientific evidence for evolution. However, as reflected by some of the comments submitted by GCSLS participants in response to this topic, many Christian educators recognize the imperative for engaging students, parents, and colleagues in open discussion of this third rail of Christian education. Participants provided feedback like, "We are failing our constituents if we don't have this discussion and have it honestly." Others pointed out the need for open dialogue with students, replying, "Embrace the questions kids ask! Allow the cognitive dissonance." Still others remarked, "We need to take a position on the fact that we can't be sure that our favorite position is the only position to take" and "Good science can help us correct bad theology and good theology can help us correct bad science." Finally, one participant pointed out, "Discussion of challenging topics requires broad preparation and a long on-ramp." Indeed, preparation and a "long on-ramp" of healthy dialogue are essential if Christian schools are going to safely grab the third rail of origins.

Why We Must Seize the Opportunity

To adequately prepare our students to be disciples of Christ in the scientific and technological world of the 21st century, we must provide them a thoughtful and honest Christian education that seeks to harmonize orthodox theology and an unwavering commitment to God's inerrant and infallible Word with good science and to do so with humility. Students must be taught that there are orthodox Christian theologians and scientists who love Christ and are committed to His Word but who have different perspectives on how to harmonize the Bible and science and how to interpret the first chapters of Genesis.

Engaging our students in an open discussion of the relationship between theology and science is critically important. When led by prayerful and mature teachers and mentors, such discussions can help to solidify students' faith in God's Word, vaccinate them against scientism and naturalistic materialism, and deepen their commitment to Jesus Christ, His Word, and the advancement of His kingdom.

Conversely, failure to engage our students in such study and honest discussion places them at risk of having their faith undermined, as well as limiting their potential to pursue STEM-related careers and being salt and light within those careers. Moreover, to explicitly assert or imply that there is only one biblically faithful perspective on cosmology, including human origins and the age of the universe, and that all other perspectives are at best misguided and at worst the root of atheism, is dangerous (even if well-intended). Doing so forecloses students' ability to think critically about origins and prevents them from learning how to grapple thoughtfully with both theology and scientific data. By implying that "my interpretation and perspective is the only biblically accurate one" and that other interpretations and perspectives of highly trained Christian theologians and scientists are de facto wrong, it also misses a valuable opportunity to demonstrate humility for our students.

How to Grab the Third Rail and Survive

Grabbing the third rail in a subway is not safe; neither is grabbing the third rail in Christian education. It is not safe for at least two reasons: (1) opening a robust discussion of Genesis and evolution in our Bible and science classrooms runs the risk of a backlash by those who will interpret such dialogue as leading down a slippery slope toward theological compromise; and (2) there is always the danger of eisegeting (misinterpreting) Scripture based on potentially false scientific theories. The risk runs two ways. This difficulty arises in part because many schools lack a robust theological underpinning for their philosophy of education, let alone science education. Compounding the problem is limited understanding of the disciplined protocols of scientific research and discovery upon which good science is built.

Humility precedes learning. Before we can move forward we must be humble enough to acknowledge that we can be wrong in our interpretations of the Bible or the world around us through science. We must also be willing to admit that we need to develop a much deeper and holistic philosophy of education—especially of science education—that is faithful to God's Word, to what is revealed in His world, and to the mission of our Christian schools.

It is important to establish clear nonnegotiable theological tenets to guide discussions. These tenets must reflect irreducible essentials of the Christian faith but must not be confused with nonessential interpretations, e.g., specific interpretations of passages in Genesis. The following fundamental theological tenets are offered for consideration as nonnegotiables:

- God created, sustains, and governs the universe.
- The God who created this world also reveals Himself to humanity through the two books of revelation: His Word and His world. (Psalm 19; John 1–3)
- God's Word is inerrant and infallible.
- The Bible is authoritative and sufficient for salvation and our only rule of faith and life.
- God is sovereign over all creation and all realms of human endeavor and has given human beings special abilities and responsibilities through the Creation Covenant and additionally in the Great Commission to believers.
- God is both transcendent and immanent.
- Adam and Eve were historical people.
- The Fall was a historical event.
- The God who created this world is also our Redeemer through Jesus Christ, the Second Adam.

How long God took to create, the mechanism He used for doing so, and how Adam and Eve became living souls are not stated as nonnegotiables. That God creates, sustains, and governs His universe, that Adam and Eve were historical beings who sinned and doomed all humanity, and that Christ, the Second Adam, redeemed fallen humanity—these are clearly nonnegotiables. It is not easy to define the nonnegotiables, and each faith tradition may vary on the specifics. However, defining them clearly but not too narrowly is essential for setting the stage for honest, robust dialogue. Doing so helps establish trust and confidence that fundamental biblical truth is not at risk. What better place to have honest, robust dialogue than within the Christian school?

Having established the nonnegotiables, it is important to recognize and acknowledge that Christian theologians and scientists do not agree on a single interpretation of Genesis. This does not mean that Christians cannot unapologetically join world-class science and a vibrant Christianity. All knowledge comes from God; students need to understand that all truth is God's truth, because all truth originates in the mind of God and is reflected in everything that He has created as well as what He has revealed to us in His Word.

As Christians, we must not only take care to avoid allowing our biases, cultural experiences, and current understandings to cause us to misinterpret (eisegete) Scripture, but also take seriously the truth that all truth is God's truth no matter who proclaims it. Because of God's general revelation and His common grace, all humans can unfold the potentialities of the created order. Because of God's special revelation and His special grace, believers can discern God's kingdom patterns in the unfolding of the created order through science. Such discernment engenders worship, acknowledging God's omniscience, omnipotence, and omnipresence.

Practical Considerations

It is one thing to gather up one's courage to grab the third rail. It is another thing to do so without being electrocuted. In order to seize the opportunity and realize the educational value of engaging in this important discussion of origins with staff, students, and parents—as well as to minimize backlash—the following guidelines will be helpful:

- Prepare yourself by reading several books and papers reflecting positions that may be different than your own regarding Genesis, the age of the earth, and how God may have created His world and human beings.

- Have the board read the above as well as other resources, invite experts to speak to the board, and engage the board in healthy discussion of why it is important to engage students in this dialogue. You may wish to have a board study committee formed to develop a position paper on the matter. If yours is a church school, church leadership must be actively engaged in the discussion and planning.

- Have the board and administration conduct town halls with parents on why the school is tackling such a sensitive and difficult issue. Explain the spiritual and academic merits of engaging in this difficult subject.

- Establish a faith/science course, or a unit of study within an existing Bible or science course, on the relationship between faith and science that includes grade-appropriate and in-depth discussions, research, and presentations on the issue of origins including different perspectives on how to interpret the first chapters of Genesis, the age of the universe and the earth, and evolution.

- Develop a multiyear and scaffolded professional development program for administrators and teachers. Encourage reading on science-related topics, celebrating the beauty and complexity of God's creation. Provide both the space for and the skills to address complex, potentially divisive issues within a context of loving community.

In these efforts, the goal for Christian school leaders and teachers is that they have a basic understanding of exegesis and hermeneutics. They should be comfortable and generally conversant with the predominant and alternative theological interpretations of Genesis and be able to contrast them with naturalistic/materialistic evolution. They should be able to communicate the purpose, goals, benefits, and parameters of the school's objectives to parents and students.

Content-area specialists should develop a deep and thorough knowledge of these views and be able to teach them effectively to their students. This includes learning how to share their particular perspectives and convictions while accurately and evenhandily presenting other views. Teachers should assign readings from original source documents related to each view, and establish a classroom climate that ensures that students feel safe to ask tough questions and to respectfully disagree (and to be assured that they will not be penalized socially or academically for articulating positions contrary to a teacher's own).

The goal for students is to develop a thoughtful and well-informed understanding of these complex issues so that they are prepared as disciples of Christ to be salt and light in this world. To achieve this goal, establish clear objectives for the faith/science and other Bible and science courses. Students need to know that good theology and good science reveal the character and work of God and enable people to fulfill His calling as God's stewards of creation. They need to know the facts, practices, and perspectives of modern natural and physical science and be able to show how Christians can address evolutionary hypotheses, theories, and philosophies. Finally, they should understand the role of STEM-related courses in fulfilling both the Cultural Mandate and the Great Commission.

Conclusion

Reconciling the first chapters of Genesis (God's written Word) with the findings of modern science regarding God's creation, and graciously and effectively dealing with these matters in the Christian school, are two "wicked" problems. A wicked problem is not evil; rather, it is highly complex. The Colossian Forum defines wicked problems this way:

> Not all problems are created equal. Some problems are tame. Tame problems can be defined, and solved to everyone's satisfaction. Get a man to the moon? Check. But not all problems are like that. Some problems are hard to define, and so hard to solve. These problems aren't tame. They're wicked, as in wicked hard.[2]

The Stanford Social and Innovation Review defines a wicked problem this way:

> A social or cultural problem that is difficult or impossible to solve for as many as four reasons: incomplete or contradictory knowledge, the number of people and opinions involved, the large economic burden, and the interconnected nature of these problems with other problems.[3]

The above definition certainly reflects the problem of dealing with origins in our Christian school classrooms! But the complexity of wicked problems is no excuse for ignoring them. As God's image bearers, we are called to be problem solvers and to engage complex issues in a manner that furthers love of God and love of neighbor. As Christian educators, we are called to teach our students to be lifelong learners and problem solvers, within the context of loving and respectful relationships.

We cannot do this if we ignore or overly simplify the problem of reconciling the first chapters of Genesis with the findings of science. This is the third rail in Christian education. It is dangerous; it is difficult; it is a "wicked" problem. It is also one that we must grab if we are to fulfill our callings before Christ and prepare our students to go forth as lights in the world.

Discussion Questions

1. When and how does your school currently engage students in discussions around the intersections of faith and science? Around origins?

2. Are those discussions sufficiently complex, and do they allow opportunity for students to engage with various theological and scientific perspectives?

3. What practical strategies can you use to harness the opportunity of discussion around origins at your school? How can your school maximize the potential of that discussion for student learning, growth, and preparation for college and career?

NOTES

1 Safire, W., "Third Rail." New York Times, February 18, 2017. http://www.nytimes.com/2007/02/18/magazine/18wwlnsafire.t.html.

2 The Colossian Way. "Wicked Problems—The Colossian Way." http://www.colossianway.org/wicked-problems/ (retrieved April 2, 2017).

3 Kolko, J. (2012). *Wicked Problems: Problems Worth Solving* (Stanford Social Innovation Review, 2012). Emphasis in original.

Chapter 5

Relevance and the Christian School Movement: A Global Perspective

Gavin Brettenny and Dan Egeler

It has been said that candlemakers did not invent the light bulb. While candle makers persisted in their craft, light bulbs became relevant and candles became ambiance. If the Christian school movement is not globally relevant, then it is not globally sustainable, outside of mood. To extend the metaphor, this chapter motivates against the idea of the Christian school movement becoming a globally unified candlemakers' guild. This movement, into which Christian educators have been called, requires leadership with competencies that enact relevance.

Relevance was a central theme that emerged at the 2017 Global Christian School Leadership Summit. This theme has been well-served by other chapters in this book, and the insights therein broadly apply to the global Christian school movement. In terms of economic sustainability, the global Christian school movement is in need of collaborative partnerships and resources that will serve to sustain momentum and that promote the development and sharing of professional and business relevance. Importantly, an entire chapter is dedicated to cultural engagement, which is a critical topic for the global movement given the cultural challenges across the world today. The same could be said for legal and legislative issues, and the other chapters as well.

This chapter's unique contribution to the concept of relevance for Christian schooling is that it examines two types of relevance that must be pursued by Christian schools everywhere: (1) educating students for relevance in the world; and (2) schools' relevance to each other, through unity

Both efforts are fundamental to the future of the global Christian school movement, on many levels. For example, this two-pronged relevance will serve to strengthen schools' sustainability and students' ability to engage with the culture.

Educating Students for Relevance in the World

Globalism and the digital global village are not birthing global uniformity, at least not beyond the superficial level of global youth popular culture, entertainment, and fashion. This is a factional world where diversity becomes more noticeable and proximity often results in intolerance and violence. Nationalism is rising in response to globalism. Ideological forces of globalization and nationalization (one world order and tribalism) vociferously compete for stage time, head space, and land. Dissonant voices are shouting "truth" in a room that seems to be getting smaller.

In the midst of these divisive ideologies is the deep problem of global inequality. Rich and poor are now, more easily than ever before, looking at each other across the same room in a shrinking world. Homeostasis through globalization is a myth. Nationalism divides. The impulse is to retreat, to escape to Jerusalem. This is not a quiet world, and the world's youth are listening. But education can build capacity to help them discern the voices—and Christian schools are on the rise in many parts of the world. In light of this, there must be wisdom guiding the education for relevance in such a fractured world. The word *wisdom* (*phronesis* in Greek) means to discern modes of action with a view to their results.

Christian education about "the world" must not ask students to make a singular binary choice between their faith and the world. Simplistic faith-based binary choices inevitably result in an "us and them" comparison and judgment, creating an immature faith that is too often the extension of human ego. The binary practice of separation and control is human religion in a worldly system. Jesus spoke strongly against this approach and the ministers of such religion (Mark 7:4–16).

Christian education should prepare students to negotiate the paradox of being in but not of the world. Being open to paradox in Scripture takes the learner beyond immature "us and them" divisions, leading to deeper spiritual insights, humility, a life that unifies across cultures, respecting difference, embracing common values, having a gentle answer, and standing in and for a biblical view of the world. Educating for the application of such a worldview is fundamental to enable students to be relevant to the world while not being of the world—an important global perspective.

When speaking about the world it is helpful for interpretation and action to understand biblical language. *The world* as a place which we should not become part of refers to *systems* that humans habitually construct: egocentric behaviors requiring security, status, pleasure, power, and most importantly, control. Evidence of these systems is often exploitation of the vulnerable. Christians are commanded not to love these human systems (1 John 2:15).

Jesus instructed His followers, "Go into all the world and preach the good news to all creation" (Mark 16:15). It is helpful to understand His careful choice of words:

1. "Go": lead over, carry over, transfer.

2. "all the world": *kosmos*, the sum of all things earthly, world affairs/systems (human constructs).

3. "preach": public proclamation.

4. "all creation": the sum of all things created—every building, every creation, every creature, every ordinance. This speaks of what God and humans have created.[1]

His challenge to go to all the world and all creation comprises the biblical view of globalism. Believers are His intermediaries, representing Him to a broken world as ambassadors to a divisive system. He makes believers relevant. As the apostle Paul writes, "All this is from God, who reconciled us to himself through Christ and gave us the ministry of reconciliation: that God was reconciling the world to himself in Christ, not counting people's sins against them. And he has committed to us the message of reconciliation" (2 Corinthians 5:18–19).

Christians are meant to sacrificially love the world as God does (John 3:16)—willing to serve as agents who bring healing and wholeness to destructive and exploitative systems, reconciling a world in crises to God. Jesus likened this approach to the penetrative qualities of the mustard seed and yeast, metaphors He used to answer the questions, "What is the kingdom of God like? What shall I compare it to?" (Luke 13:18) and, "What shall I compare the kingdom of God to?" (Luke 13:18, 20).

Christians, as the good yeast in the world, are not asked to bake a separate loaf of bread to feed the world. Good yeast works from the inside out by becoming one with or part of the life of the bread. Leavening requires Christlike character traits such as patience and humility. A God of love asks believers to become part of His world in a deep and relevant way, bringing nourishment to people in need. Christian action through education is like preparing the good yeast for infusion into the secular world. These are the followers of Christ who put into practice what the Lord commanded in Isaiah 58:6–8.

True faith matures believers, who are then enabled to live beyond the fragility of their human ego, enabling them to respond to the world's systems with love, grace, and wisdom, bringing liberty rather than mere self-serving certainty and evasive reaction. Such mature faith is on display when Jesus teaches that we are to represent Him in ways that are counter to the self-serving ways of the world, by loving our enemies (Matthew 5:43–48). By contrast, religion without personal transformation creates sectarian people who know what they are against, but too often have a poor sense of what they are for. They are portrayed as rigid, judgmental, and unhappy people reliant on public affirmation of their righteousness rather than caring about the people around them.

Instead, believers are in need of transforming faith that "runs toward the mess" in a way that is both charitable and influential. These are the many faces of true believers who are martyrs, industrialists, CEOs, technicians, farmers, homemakers, etc. They are everywhere and anywhere. They do not mind if their faith is at the center or on the margins in their societal sphere of influence. Their influence is not concerned with personal triumphalism. Their influence is about healing for the nations.

This biblical view of relevance informs an understanding of the types of graduates Christian schools must seek to prepare. One of the key activities of Christian schools should be to nurture in students their capacity for meaningful relationship. The original blessing in Genesis is a story of love and redemption through relationship, and the purpose is reconciliation of relationships with the concomitant effect of blessing on "the world." The original blessing was found in relationships: (1) between people; (2) between people and God; (3) between people and creation; and (4) within each person in terms of understanding his or her glory as God's image. Every school subject falls into one of these four relationships. History speaks of human relationships; natural sciences of our relationship with the physical universe; human sciences of our understanding of ourselves; religious instruction and Bible courses of people's relationship with God. Integrating a biblical worldview of relationship into school subject content across all ages is a learned teaching skill and a redemptive act.

In addition to cultivating students' capacity for relationship, motivational direction for learning is important, because people are not designed to find meaning in learning alone. Rather, revelatory truth gives meaning for learning. Without good teachers who provide direction, students can keep learning but never come to a knowledge of the truth (2 Timothy 3:7). Providing this personal direction is a front-end issue for the Christian school. With revelation from God, truth comes to learning. The image bearer/student encounters the Father close enough to receive the breath of life and begins to breathe eternally in the world.

Schools with no plan to translate a Kingdom worldview into teaching and learning unintentionally separate secular and sacred. Young people with Christian hearts and secular minds live with an uneducated tension that too often results in harmful Christian practice in the world. Thus this biblical view gives direct application of all knowledge taught in schools.

Relevance to Each Other: Unity

The first part of this chapter dealt with perspectives on how schools can educate students for relevance in the world. This part of the chapter addresses perspectives on Christian schools' relevance to each other around the world. This is a relational matter in the midst of a deeply relational faith. The global Christian schooling movement is experiencing exponential growth, and with it is emerging a global sense of unity across Christian schools.

This growing unity, and its impact, can be illustrated through two accounts—one from Africa, and one from Asia. First, a number of years ago, Dr. Samson Makhado, a black South African, began to share his life experience of forgiveness and reconciliation. The most poignant vignette took place when Samson was studying in Canada. His eldest son, a farmworker, died from injuries after being run over by a tractor driven by a white farmer. Samson was not immediately able to return to South Africa to bury his son due to the tense situation in the racially charged apartheid South Africa of that time. Samson was angry and bitter, and some of God's people decided to provide an opportunity for him and his wife, Mavis, to connect and heal in Europe. During a two-week period, God taught Samson the lessons of true forgiveness and to release the poison of resentment and bitterness. At the very first Christian schooling roundtable in Burkina Faso, Samson shared some of this story; unbeknownst to him, there had been a history of resentment, division, and bitterness among the Christian leaders in that country. After hearing his story, the Holy Spirit moved in a powerful way and a wave of confession and forgiveness swept through the meeting hall, leaving unity in its wake. Today, a fledgling Christian schooling movement has been launched from this initial meeting.

Second, and during the Global Christian School Leadership Summit, one of the key leaders in the Chinese "house church" Christian schooling movement sought out the speaker immediately after the opening evening's keynote address. During that address, the Chinese leader was so overwhelmed by the sense of God's presence that he stated that he could "smell God in the air." He explained that the Chinese secret service understands the threat of the house church Christian schooling movement, and has hatched a plan to combat it by sowing seeds of division and disunity among the Chinese Christian school leaders. Their attempts include using social media to foster innuendo and rumors within the leadership of the movement. This Chinese leader said that "we need this same message of unity in our country," and that he desires to hold a similar conference in China in 2018, as they are truly stronger when they stand together.

Both of these accounts illustrate the interdependency between Christian school leaders across the globe and reflect a scriptural reality. Scripture teaches that "in Christ we, though many, form one body, and each member belongs to all the others" (Romans 12:5) and that Christ is the head of the body who holds all things together (Colossians 1:17–18). As members of the same body, Christian school leaders are in great need of the encouragement and equipping that come from unity. This is true both for leaders in developing nations (where resources and know-how are often scarce) and for leaders in economically wealthy nations (which are increasingly facing moral bankruptcy). Both sets of leaders share challenges, though their settings may be different. And as members of the body of Christ, they are called to stand together, with schools nearby as well as with those across the globe.

When looking at the state of the world and the Christian school movement, there is a cultural moment in Scripture that is instructive. Specifically, there is a biblical account where God's people had just suffered a crushing defeat and found themselves surrounded by a culture that felt deeply alien. Feeling disoriented and disillusioned, they were coming under increasing pressure from society and state to compromise their unique identity and life as followers of the one true God and to embrace the relativistic and morally diverse surrounding culture.

This describes Judah following its conquest by the Chaldean emperor Nebuchadnezzar at the beginning of the Babylonian captivity. But these words come uncomfortably close to describing the realities of Christian schooling in many countries around the world today.

In biblical times, God raised up young leaders who were just teenagers; Daniel, Shadrach, Meshach, and Abednego demonstrated that it's possible to not just survive but to flourish during trying times. The key to the global future of Christian education is how to educate Daniels for sustained relevance—Daniels who would flourish in modern Babylons by not hunkering down or retreating but by "running toward the mess." Daniel did not attempt to escape from this hostile culture, but rather strove to be equipped with God's truth to engage the culture. His example rings true today and serves as a model for the new generation of Daniels as he lived faithfully and fruitfully in exile.

There are four key threads in Daniel's life that both young people today and the Christian schools that educate them can embrace:

1. Recognize that God is sovereign and, even today, believers know the end of the story. Daniel had a calm certainty that God remained sovereign and was at work for good. Daniel knew the end of the story and would not be dissuaded.

2. Focus on their true identity. Daniel focused on maintaining his identity in the midst of a culture and state aggressively seeking to co-opt it. Although he was required to take on a Babylonian name, Daniel (meaning "God is my Judge") retained his identity.

3. Demonstrate principled prudence. Daniel demonstrated profound wisdom in knowing when and how to effectively engage an unfriendly culture. He did this with creativity while proposing a different solution with eating food that he felt would defile his body. He was careful in engaging those in authority with respect. He was consistent as even his enemies could find no fault with him unless it had to do with the laws of his own God. He lived in community as he was devoted to his three young friends—Shadrach, Meshach, and Abednego. He was courageous as he was willing to face death through the lions' den rather than compromise his convictions.

4. Engage in consistent and meaningful prayer. Above all, Daniel was a man of prayer. He was consistently on his knees humbly before God, and was willing to be thrown into the lions' den rather than compromising his prayer life.

The challenge for each Christian school will be how to operationalize the lessons of Daniel's faith and life of relevance into their curricula and programs. (Certainly, the motivation for relevance must be at the front-end of schools' missions, and not tagged on the back-end through token projects or outreaches.) As a movement, Christian schools can again draw upon the strength of unity to share promising practices in educating for relevance. By preparing graduates who are ready to engage their cultures and their world, Christian schools strengthen their relevance not only for the global movement and to each other, but most importantly, to the gospel.

Discussion Questions

1. What is my school currently doing to prepare students for relevance in the world, as well as pursue unity with the global Christian school movement?

2. In what ways could my Christian school more effectively equip young people to become the good yeast in the world?

3. How could my Christian school more effectively practice unity with the global Christian school movement?

NOTES

1 Definitions taken from James Strong, *The New Strong's Expanded Exhaustive Concordance of the Bible* (Nashville, TN: Thomas Nelson; Expanded edition, 2010).

Chapter 6

Governing and Leading the Christian School: A Community-Based Approach

Paul Campey and James Drexler

In the first chapter of Genesis, God says, "Let us make mankind in our image, in our likeness" and "It is not good for the man to be alone" (Genesis 1:26a, 2:18a). From these two texts is derived "the biblical command for people to live, work, and serve in relationship with one another, reflecting the eternal relationships within the Trinity. Simply put, human beings are created, designed, and purposed to thrive and grow in the context of community. It's as much a part of the original creational order as the sun, moon, and stars, the cycle of seasons, marriage, or any of the other norms of creation."[1]

Stanley Grenz asserts, "community—or more fully stated, persons-in-relationship—is the central, organizing concept of theological construction, the theme around which a systematic theology is structured."[2] Therefore, building godly, grace-filled relationships and community must become one of the most important goals of the Christian school: "The vision is, first, that the school will be a community, a place full of adults and students who care about, look after, and root for one another and who work together for the good of the whole, in times of need and in times of celebration."[3] As was discussed in the various sessions at the 2017 Global Christian School Leadership Summit (GCSLS), and as this chapter will argue, building collaborative and trusting community within the Christian school must be a priority for both governance and leadership if Christian schooling is to flourish in the 21st century.

Community-Based Governance

Effective governance in Christian schools has not been researched to the same degree as leadership. In fact, though most school leaders can identify when governance (through the school board) is not working, it is harder to identify when the board is being proactive and assisting the school through good community-based governance that contributes to the effectiveness of the school. So the inclusion of governance as a topic at GCSLS was a critical step in assisting school boards in particular with becoming "good" boards that contribute positively to the effectiveness of their schools.

Community-based governance occurs at the local level, with people who form part of the school community governing the organization through a local board. It is not a corporate board nor is the governance removed from the operations of the school (i.e., they are not all independent board members). They are part of the community, complete with good and bad aspects—just like being part of a church family has its good and bad aspects—when it comes to governing and making sometimes hard decisions.

There were four key themes that emerged from GCSLS that were explored at each of the sessions on governance: (1) clarity; (2) stewardship; (3) relationships; and (4) trust. These topics were each grounded in biblical truth, but were also explored in a pragmatic way based on experience and case studies. They are each presented here, with the hope they can foster further discussion among readers' boards in terms of how to make a greater contribution to schools' effectiveness.

Clarity

A lack of clarity is a significant factor that undermines good community-based governance. Right from the outset a board needs to keep in mind the Scripture, "So give your servant a discerning heart to govern your people and to distinguish between right and wrong. For who is able to govern this great people of yours?" (1 Kings 3:9). This is Solomon's prayer, as the wisest man in the Bible. If his prayer was to be a servant with a discerning heart, then perhaps that is where boards (and individual board members) should start! It is often easy to get caught up in the moment, working through an issue or seeking to come up with an answer without pulling back and asking for that discerning heart and looking at an issue from a broader perspective.

Apart from seeking this discernment, considering the mode of governance used by a board is important. There are three main modes of governance for a board: fiduciary, strategic, and generative[4]. It is easy for a board to focus solely on its fiduciary role (i.e., approving budgets, reviewing actual results, and making sure compliance is up-to-date). If that is all a board does, it is not helping the school become more effective nor is it really governing the school in the full sense of the word. Boards also need to engage in strategic governance, where they react to current needs and look for prospective opportunities through strategic planning and action, as well as generative governance, where they engage in reflection and creative thinking about meaning and purpose. Effective boards are able to operate in all three of these modes and do so at the appropriate moments.

There are a few key questions to ask to diagnose board function. For example, does the board make strategic decisions or on occasion act generatively? Does the board really help management? Does it guide, does it think through issues from perhaps a different paradigm, and does it seek God's leading and guidance? Are the roles and decisions clear? Do the school leaders know where the school is headed, or does confusion reign over the school? This question is key, as a lack of clarity for the board can readily translate right through the school's day-to-day operations.

Stewardship

In many ways, the board is the ultimate steward-leader for a school. It is not only looking after the wealth that belongs to others (tuition, fees, land, buildings, assets) but also has oversight over the educational future of the students that attend that school. The board is truly a trustee. For most individual board members, the school was in existence before they joined the board, and hopefully will continue after they finish their time on the board. It is worth a board keeping this in mind as they lead the school forward—"they are standing on the shoulders of giants," just as others will also stand on their shoulders and decisions in the future.

As a steward of another's assets, the board needs to also heed the words of the parable of the talents as told in Matthew 25:14–30. It is not just about "playing it safe" but about using the assets they have for the school's best. The board must be a good steward, not just a protector of assets. They also must not be reckless with the assets or behave with them as they might their own; instead, they need to put themselves in the Master's shoes.

Relationships

Schools are relational enterprises from start to finish. As a result, the relationships between key stakeholders become critical for the good governance of a school, particularly one that has a community focus to it. The Community Governance Framework[5] highlights the centrality of four relationships: moral owners and the board; board and personnel; personnel and beneficiaries; and beneficiaries and moral owners.

The difficulty in many schools is that the same person can be in different relationships with the same people. For example, a head of school (as personnel) could also have children in the schools (as a beneficiary) and also attend the church that the school is a ministry of (as a moral owner). A head of school attends board meetings and maybe even votes (as part of the board). All of these relationships can be very confusing and open to abuse unless individuals are careful their different roles are well understood (not just by them) and it is clearly worked out how the relationships are to work.

Assuming that appropriate boundaries are set, like all healthy relationships, the relationships need to be two-way, with deliberate steps taken to sustain these relationships. If the relationships are not deliberately two-way, they will slowly wither and become unhealthy. Healthy relationships make for a healthy organization, which in turn make a healthy mission and purpose more achievable.

Trust

Trust is really the basis upon which strong relationships are founded. Trust needs to start at the top between the board chair and the head of school, and then infect all levels of the school board and on into management and the day-to-day operations of the school. A lack of trust at the top can be felt throughout the school. And once trust is lost it is very hard to restore. It takes time and effort, humbling oneself in the errors made, and may even take a change in people (board and/or school leaders) before trust can be restored.

It is therefore critical that the board work hard to create and maintain a culture of trust for the whole school organization, to better achieve the ends it sets out for the whole school. Actions that a board and school leadership can take to create trust include the following:

• Not being overly defensive

• Not creating surprises for the other party

• Having respect for and trust in the other party (right from the start)

• Being consistent in decision making

• Being straight with the truth (even when it is bad news)

• Not being prideful

• Not being unprofessional

From a board perspective, it is essential that board look after their heads of school, but also give them appropriate feedback and timely appraisal. In fact, some argue that the relationship between the board and school leadership is the most important, and one that requires intentional and constant attention. A poor relationship between the board and head of school will translate directly into organizational uncertainty, which leads down the path of confusion and ultimately ineffectiveness.

This section of the chapter has focused on a community-based view of one side of this two-way relationship (the board); the next section of this chapter will focus specifically on leadership. Both sides are essential for school health.

Community-Based Leadership

The inaugural Global Christian School Leadership Summit was centered, in part, on how best to guide, direct, and administer schools. Several sessions were devoted to varying aspects of effective leadership, with a view toward models and practices that not only reflect biblical principles but also provide the best possible education for students. Among the characteristics for Christian school leadership that emerged from GCSLS, and that are supported in the literature on best practices, are the following:

• *Relational.* As discussed in the preceding section on governance, schools are communities, clusters of individuals who can either work in isolation or in collaborative interdependence with one another. The entrenched habits of individualism and competition that characterize most Christian schools are antithetical to the teaching of Paul: "The eye cannot say to the hand, 'I have no need of you,' nor again the head to the feet, 'I have no need of you'" (1 Corinthians 12:21, ESV). The various gifts given to God's people are "for the common good" (1 Corinthians 12:7), and God's design is that "there may be no division in the body" (1 Corinthians 12:25). Paul is writing about the church, but this consistent biblical teaching on community, relationship, and collaboration must compel our Christian schools towards relational teaching, learning, and leadership.

- *Missional/Cultural.* Everything that happens in the school must be aligned with the mission and purposes of the school. The mission of the school should be clear and concise, referred to for all curricular and cocurricular decisions, and published broadly in publications, documents, and wall posters. The culture of Christian schools is critically important. Culture means the norms, beliefs, values, rituals, and practices of the school—all of which help to define "how we do it here." The culture must flow from and be consistent with the mission of the school; in fact, one of the chief tasks of leadership according to Thomas Sergiovanni is for the leader to "express outrage" when practices or policies are in contradiction to the mission and culture of the school[6].

- *Adaptable.* Schools are communities, but these communities are composed of multiple individuals, changing situations, and differing contexts, so leadership must adapt to each situation to be effective.[7]

- *Incarnational.* According to Van Brummelen, "The overall aim of Christian schooling is to help students be and become responsive disciples of Jesus Christ."[8] The shepherding and disciple-making role of Christian leaders, therefore, is paramount. James Davison Hunter argues for the "faithful presence" of Christians in their work and communities, and this presence is in essence incarnational: "For the Christian, if there is a possibility for human flourishing in a world such as ours, it begins when God's word of love becomes flesh in us, is embodied in us, is enacted through us...."[9] Leadership in this regard is centered on discipleship and spiritual formation.

- *Developmental* (Shared). This is at the crux of Christian school leadership as leaders intentionally and proactively share the leadership, power, and authority (other authors refer to "distributed leadership," "collaborative leadership," "shared leadership," "cultural leadership," and "servant leadership") with the other professionals in the building. As Michael Fullan argues, "the indelible leader is to develop collaborative cultures . . . to the point where you become dispensable to your group."[10] Indelible leadership develops "deep leaders," and leaders upon leaders, which is the potential legacy of "Distributed and Developmental Leadership."

While these are widely recognized characteristics of successful school leadership, schools are fairly conservative places when it comes to change, and human beings generally like the ease and comfort of what is familiar and routine. So, despite moving into a new century with globalization, a technology and information revolution, automation, demographic shifts, and other significant changes, most schools still operate with structures, schedules, and leadership that have roots in the last century or earlier (e.g., a nine-month school year and dividing students by age). Key questions Christian educators must ask are, How can Christian school leadership be improved? How can that leadership help teachers and students? How can leadership increase learning outcomes?

These questions—and characteristics for leaders—point Christian school leaders to one of the most crucial roles they play: instructional leaders. The reason for this is that, as Hargreaves and Fullan explain, "There is widespread agreement now that of all the factors inside the school that affect children's learning and achievement, the most important is the teacher— not standards, assessments, resources, or even the school's leadership, but the quality of the teacher. Teachers really matter."[11] As the authors later assert, school leaders must learn that professional development for faculty can "never be done to or even for teachers," but achieved best and most deeply by and with them.[12] This represents a monumental shift in how Christian educators have historically thought about schools and leadership.

The question becomes how school leaders can foster an effective instructional culture. One useful lens through which to consider this question is again offered by Hargreaves and Fullan, who borrow the economic principle of capital and apply it to schooling in describing the three parts of professional capital: *human*, *social*, and *decisional*. Just like money, professional capital must be circulated and shared to be most effective.

Human capital means the skills, knowledge, expertise, experience, and talents of each individual teacher in the school, as well as skills like knowing the subject, knowing and using a variety of pedagogical strategies, understanding how children learn, understanding the unique culture of the school and school families, and having the passion and commitment to help students learn. Each teacher has some level of human capital, but in most schools this capital is not circulated, invested, or shared with others; educators commonly work in isolation most of the day. As instructional leaders, school leaders have the responsibility to foster the professional growth of their teachers, as well as reduce their isolation.

Second, social capital is how "the quantity and quality of interactions and social relationships among people affects their access to knowledge and information."[13] Social capital is a collective capacity that exists as teachers have the time, space, and authority to interact recurrently about teaching and learning. In short, the sum is always worth more than the individual parts. In schools where social capital is strong (implying a high degree of trust, strong relationships, and consequential conversations about learning), improvements and innovations can advance. The good news is that when social capital is strong, human capital improves, teachers grow, student achievement increases, and the faculty stay for years. For these reasons, school leaders must attend to relationships, as emphasized throughout this chapter.

Third, Hargreaves and Fullan describe decisional capital. Simply put, decisional capital is the ability and authority to make discretionary judgments even where there are no fixed rules. Decisional capital is sharpened through social capital, and is accumulated through experience, reflection, and collaboration. It calls for shared or distributed leadership among the professionals in the school. This has profound implications for the way school leaders facilitate (versus make) decisions regarding curriculum, testing, students, special programs, and so forth.

In the past 20 years or so, a new structure for schooling has emerged, a framework now commonly known as professional learning communities (PLCs), that allows for all three forms of professional capital to flourish. PLCs are not the newest educational method to try, nor another thing to add to everyone's busy schedule, but an entirely different way to design and lead schools.[14] It is beyond the scope of this chapter to describe all the details of how PLCs work and the benefits they provide to schools, but PLCs become the professional development of the faculty as they learn to regularly collaborate, share, and lead. As this happens, research shows that student achievement increases and the load of leadership on the principal or head of school is lessened as educators move from "teaching" to "learning."

PLCs emanate from the view that schools are fundamentally communities, where all constituents—including the board, school leaders, teachers, parents, and students—are engaged in common goals and the work of learning, together. Although educational change is always difficult, a healthy future for Christian education will necessitate re-envisioning school governance and leadership—and even schools themselves—from a community-based perspective. This reflects a growing understanding among Christian school educators that this view of schools leads to better outcomes for students, and a healthier climate in which educators can themselves flourish.

Discussion Questions:

1. Which of the characteristics for community-based governance (clarity, stewardship, relationships, and trust) are the most well-developed among your board? Which need the most work by the board, and what steps in that direction should be taken?

2. What training, reading, and discussion is being undertaken by your school board, so that it becomes a more effective board and therefore has great impact on your school?

3. Which of the characteristics for Christian school leadership (relational, missional, cultural, adaptable, incarnational, developmental) are the most important for you and your school? Why?

4. What changes would you and your school have to make in order to implement a professional learning community in your school?

NOTES

1 James L. Drexler, *Nurturing the School Community: Teacher Induction and Professional Learning Communities* (Colorado Springs, CO: Purposeful Design Publications, 2011), 9.

2 Stanley Grenz, *Renewing the Center: Evangelical Theology in a Post-Theological Era* (Grand Rapids: Baker Books, 2000), 214–215.

3 Roland Barth, "The Culture Builder," *Educational Leadership* 59 (8) (2002): 6–11.

4 Richard Chait, Ryan William, and Barbara Taylor, *Governance as Leadership: Reframing the Work of Nonprofit Boards* (Hoboken, NJ: John Wiley & Sons, 2011).

5 David Bartlett and Paul Campey, *Community Governance—A Framework for Building Healthy Christian Organizations* (Gosford, Australia: Resolve Consulting, 2008).

6 Thomas Sergiovanni, *Moral Leadership: Getting to the Heart of School Improvement* (San Francisco: Jossey-Bass, 1992), 74, 130.

7 Blanchard and Hersey developed their "Situational Leadership" model in the 1980s; Heifetz and Laurie proposed their "Adaptive Leadership" in the 1990s; both approaches seem to build on the "Contingency Leadership" theories of Fred Fiedler, and each emphasizes adaptability to the situation and person.

8 Harro Van Brummelen, *Walking with God in the Classroom: Christian Approaches to Teaching and Learning* (Colorado Springs, CO: Purposeful Design Publications, 2009).

9 James Davidson Hunter, *To Change the World: The Irony, Tragedy, and Possibility of Christianity in the Late Modern World* (New York: Oxford University Press, 2010), 241.

10 Michael Fullan, *Indelible Leadership: Always Leave Them Learning* (Thousand Oaks, California: Corwin, 2017), 63.

11 Andy Hargreaves and Michael Fullan, *Professional Capital: Transforming Teaching in Every School* (New York: Teachers College Press, 2012), xii, emphasis added.

12 Ibid., 45.

13 Ibid., 90.

14 Readers can learn more about how PLCs work and how they can improve learning, enhance professionalism, and transform their schools in *Nurturing the School Community* by James L. Drexler, and by consulting www.allthingsplc.info, the home for Solution Tree, the experts in PLCs.

Chapter 7

Religious Liberties and a Faithful Christian Presence: Responding to Legal and Legislative Issues in Christian Education

Mark Spencer and Philip Scott

> My goal is that they may be encouraged in heart and united in love, so that they may have the full riches of complete understanding, in order that they may know the mystery of God, namely, Christ, in whom are hidden all the treasures of wisdom and knowledge. (Colossians 2:2–3, NIV)

The banner verse for the 2017 Global Christian School Leadership Summit, written all those years ago to the Colossian church, remains as relevant to this final chapter as the very first and all those in between. As courts and legislators look at Christian education, they are often mystified by Christian educators' actions and fail to see the hidden treasures of wisdom and knowledge they bring. Instead, often more from ignorance than malice, a judge or legislator will act according to the prevailing culture and societal norms, doing what is "right in his own eyes" (Judges 17:6, NASB), and reacting to those with the loudest voices or positions of influence. However as a movement, Christian education must respond in unity and love to the legal and legislative challenges of the day.

These challenges were front and center at GCSLS. Themes that emerged included the critical importance of establishing the religious character of educational ministries in foundational documents, and then consistently reinforcing that character in subsequent policies, forms, and communication materials. While Christians often emphasize relationship over rules, the legal system looks first at rules and documentation to understand and define relationships, providing a very real challenge to the way many ministries operate.

On the legislative side, participants discussed practical ways to speak into and influence the legislative process, by building relationships with all levels of government and not shying away from engagement with elected officials. These relationships help to put a "face to a name" when elected officials are working on legislation that affects Christian education and Christian educators. Many of those present commented on the importance of working with and being supported by broader associations in these endeavors.

Religious Liberties and a Faithful Christian Presence:
Responding to Legal and Legislative Issues in Christian Education

59

Another important area was related to Sexual Orientation and Gender Identity (SOGI) rights, which are increasingly being asserted—in many cases in ways that conflict with long held religious freedom rights. While focusing on the immediate context of the U.S., the issues and challenges are the same across most Western nations. Firsthand examples were provided from Canadian schools of SOGI rights being supported through government mandates. The progression of culture in the U.S. was posed as a looming threat to Christian institutions and as an opportunity to revisit what the gospel of Christ actually requires of us and what are the impediments we have added to the gospel. Participant responses overwhelmingly identified the need to prepare and get on the front foot in understanding the changing times and how to respond authentically. Again, the importance of documentation came to the fore; as one participant put it, ministries need to be "making sure our ducks are in a row and not swimming all over the pond!"

The need for more research and understanding of the issues involved was also identified by participants, particularly with regard to LGBTIQA+ issues (this nomenclature seeks to incorporate together descriptors relating to sexual orientation, lesbian, gay, bisexual, asexual; gender identity, transgender, queer; biological status, intersex; together with '+' as a symbol of inclusivity). Participants were challenged to question which male/female norms they hold as central to male/female distinctives, and to parse out which are just cultural preferences or truly reflective of immutable male/female characteristics grounded in Scripture.

Throughout these presentations ran a thread that if pulled and examined exposes two separate but related concerns. The first concern was the issue of defining who Christian schools and institutions are from a legal perspective and with an eye, at least in Western countries, to explicitly making known their religious beliefs. Those explicit claims of faith-based operations currently can serve as a legal protection, even if it may be a societal liability. As it relates to this aspect the focus was on building legal walls to protect schools.

Likely more important was the second concern, which also centered on Christian schools and institutions defining who they are but from the perspective of ministerial and theological aspects. This means that educators were challenged to be introspective of what they really believe and what the essential elements of their faith are, and what are preferences that may be laid aside in order to reach more families and students (or more effectively reach the families and students they already serve). In this context schools are actually breaking down walls in order to carry out their purposes.

In reality these are not two concerns but two aspects of the same concern. The key legal and legislative question facing Christian educators is, "How do we define who we are both internally to our community and externally to the watching world?" In part, one requires a legal response and in part, one requires a ministerial response. There is wisdom in not confusing the two, or assuming if schools can resolve one concern, they have resolved both. The remainder of this chapter seeks to address both parts of this question, first by considering the space occupied by Christian education in society, then by describing the approaches Christian educators can take in response, and finally, by offering a list of resources of help to Christian educators in this arena.

Legal and Legislative "Space"

Underpinning each of the legal and legislative discussions at GCSLS are theological and cultural understandings of the church and Christian education and their place in society. Western democracies are, by and large, built on the liberal democratic tradition, emphasizing personal freedoms, liberty, and defined roles for government. Within this tradition religious freedom is one of the classic freedoms and the basis for the establishment of churches, Christian schools, Christian colleges and universities, and other Christian ministries. On that foundation, much of the emphasis in the U.S., Canada, and Australia is focused on preserving and protecting existing freedoms, or carving out a legal and legislative "space" for a Christian school or educational ministry to operate. Just as a physical space is needed for a school, a legal and legislative space is needed within a society where a Christian school or institution can express its faith freely and openly. Just as work is needed to build the physical spaces (and funding needed as well!) there is also the need to invest in creating the legal and legislative space.

The legal and legislative space for a Christian school or institution is effectively determined by the legislation or court rulings that either prescribe actions to be taken or, conversely, prohibit actions being taken. Legislation or court determinations are not fixed and immutable but change over time, merely reflecting a point-in-time codification of the values and beliefs of a society and its culture. Government and laws are nothing if not a moral proclamation. Courts, and more directly, legislators are not immune to these changes in values and beliefs. Indeed, for legislators, their role is largely about understanding, if not also helping to form and shape, those societal values and beliefs. While judicial officers have traditionally claimed greater impartiality, they cannot operate in a values vacuum, and often legislation will require consideration of "accepted community standards" in the making of a judgment.

Historically the values and beliefs which underpinned Western cultures were Judeo-Christian values, and the laws made by legislatures and the decisions of the court, to a greater or lesser degree, reflected these values. These values and beliefs are rapidly changing in the U.S. Similar, if not greater, changes are occurring in Canada, Australia, and many other Western nations. Many of these changes in societal values are also being reflected, albeit to a lesser degree in some cases, in values amongst professing Christians. Returning to the "space" metaphor, the boundaries for that legal and legislative space in the West are thus being increasingly determined on the basis of values and beliefs that are antithetical to traditional Judeo-Christian values. In addition, what may once have been fairly rigid boundaries are becoming increasingly permeable as more and more of those within the Church, and thus the Christian school or institution, are sharing those commonly held societal values.

It is no longer possible to assume that the values and beliefs espoused within Christian schools and institutions are held by those in courts or legislatures. While those involved in Christian education may accept that "The fear of the Lord is the beginning of wisdom" (Proverbs 9:10), this phrase may not receive a positive response in the wider community.

Religious Liberties and a Faithful Christian Presence:
Responding to Legal and Legislative Issues in Christian Education

61

In some cases it is clear they are not, and in fact those values and beliefs are likely to be increasingly contested within a given school community and possibly even within staff. It cannot even be assumed that language is necessarily understood across the generations within the church and school community, let alone outside this environment (e.g., different generational understandings of the historical gay rights movement versus the current LGBTIQA+ movement).

It is recognized that in many other parts of the world this space is far more constrained or, indeed, not formally recognized at all. In those contexts, the legal and legislative challenges are likely to focus not on the protection of these spaces but on establishing legal rights and legislation that provides for some form of recognition or acceptance in the first place. While reflecting a different starting point, many of the practical challenges and solutions that follow in this chapter are still likely to be relevant.

Christian Education's Response

Christian schools and institutions have choices to make in the face of this changing world. The choices could be labeled as "protectionist" or "missional." Each can find a basis in Scripture, and either can be a faithful response by an individual Christian school or other educational ministry to God's plan and the leading of the Holy Spirit. As with any dichotomous characterization, these choices have the potential to become caricatures of what has been described. While the reality for Christian schools and institutions will be far more complex than these two choices can encompass, they serve as useful illustrative tools and means of categorizing potential responses.

A protectionist approach, as the name implies, would see Christian schools and institutions focusing on ensuring that within that school community there is a strong reinforcement of beliefs and values. Perpetuation of faith and maintenance of existing religious freedom based largely on claims to those freedoms becomes the dominant paradigm of engagement with the legal and legislative environment. Of course, this approach can only be sustained against the background of strong existing religious freedoms and with an eye to protecting those freedoms.

A missional approach requires a change of mind-set for many Christian schools and institutions in the West. While still ensuring there is a strong reinforcement of beliefs and values within that school community, a missional approach necessitates that Christian educators begin to live and think as minorities. This requires engaging with society in winsome, diplomatic ways. In this approach, Christian educators must operate with the assumption that their actions and motives are understood as bad for society and bad for individuals—and in some cases even evil. Christian educators cannot give those who hold a different view a basis to criticize them through the use of careless language or by unthinking behavior, but will need to be explicit in explanations of why they do what they do, and ensure their students and families also understand these rationales.

From a global perspective, it is important to note that outside the West, with its traditions of protection of religious freedoms, these choices may be reflected differently. In countries where the Christian faith is either merely tolerated, or, worse, actively persecuted, a "protectionist" approach to the legal and legislative environment may be less about protecting existing freedoms as much as actively working to keep out of the public sphere, avoiding attention, and operating in the "grey areas" often found just outside the law. A "missional" approach in these contexts would be similar to that in the West, i.e., operating as a minority and seeking to win favor as a means of gaining, in this case, increased freedom.

One of the most obvious areas where religious freedoms and the prevailing culture have conflicted over the years has been in relation to sexuality. Most evangelical Christians would agree that the Bible clearly confines sexual expression within the bounds of a marriage relationship between a man and a woman. The prevailing cultural views in this area have shifted dramatically from the 1960s, when a far more "laissez-faire" approach to heterosexual sexual activity outside marriage was adopted. Subsequently views on homosexual activity also changed, and this became more acceptable within society generally. This has been reflected in a wide range of legislative changes and court decisions across many Western nations. Initial legislative reforms focused on decriminalization of homosexual activity, with more recent changes based around nondiscrimination principles seeking to provide equal rights to same-sex relationships in relation to property rights, adoption and surrogacy, or recognition of relationships as marriages.

More recently the cultural focus has shifted away from merely sexual activity or even sexual orientation to "gender identity," with Sexual Orientation and Gender Identity (SOGI) rights being asserted across a wide range of areas. The dominant cultural narrative understands "gender" to be distinct from [biological] sex with individuals able to determine their own "gender identity" independently from their sex "assigned at birth."[1] On the basis of this self-determined gender, individuals then claim the right to be treated as if their sex correlated with their gender. This can be in the form of adopting the social markers traditionally associated with a particular sex, such as dress and school uniforms, and on through to access to facilities such as changing rooms and bathrooms. Failure to accept this cultural narrative is being equated in the public square with racist attitudes of the past and linked with increased rates of suicide and negative mental health outcomes. Indeed, against the background of a wave of activism in this area, Christian education is in danger of being characterized by what it stands against, rather than what it stands for.

Yet in the midst of these challenging circumstances there is hope. Christian schools and institutions across the globe educate millions of young people on a daily basis. Christian education doesn't merely provide academic instruction but seeks to form young people in the knowledge of the fullness of Christ—young people who understand their identity in the revelation of Christ's love for them and His saving grace. Christian schools and institutions have an incredible opportunity to speak into these young lives. As such, they should strive to become known for their positive oddities and not their perceived condemnations of society or individuals. If the Christian education movement is faithful to Christ it should

Religious Liberties and a Faithful Christian Presence:
Responding to Legal and Legislative Issues in Christian Education

63

look and operate differently than its counterparts. Those differences need to be explained to legal authorities and community and should reflect the love of Christ. In this way, Christian schools and institutions can begin to rebuild their reputations and show they are for the common good of the community and not out for their own preservation, even in spite of some actions and beliefs that might be interpreted as odd or even negative.

A Practical Plan of Action

The clear messages from GCSLS reflect a plan of action to ensure that Christian educators have the legal and legislative space to continue their work. This plan starts with establishing sound theological underpinnings for their actions. Policies and practices must flow from biblically based beliefs, not mere prejudices or cultural conventions. Christian educators need to be willing to examine what they do in the light of Scripture. Further, on the basis of sound theology, Christian educators need to undertake practical research and thought on the application of these biblical truths. The feedback from many GCSLS participants called for more frontline research and thinking on what is actually being claimed in the current cultural narratives, how that compares with biblical truth, and how this may impact practices within Christian schools and institutions.

In order to embed these practices Christian schools and institutions need to ensure their written documents truly reflect the totality of who they are and what they believe. Faith, values, and beliefs should be captured and evidenced in foundational documents, policies, and practices, as that will be the basis upon which Christian schools and institutions will be judged, to a large degree. This is of particular importance in the area of employment.

With a clear understanding of what they believe and why, and policies and practices to reflect this, Christian schools and institutions will have a sound footing on which to develop relationships with legislators. While legislators may not always agree with the positions proposed, communicating with them and helping them to understand the truth of who Christian educators are and what they are seeking has an enormous impact on legislation. The political world is the modern day "city gates," at which Christian educators need to engage in discussions with civic leaders. This engagement needs to happen at all levels of government, and Christian educators need to have the wisdom to know when to engage and when not to engage on an issue.

Some Christian schools and institutions may be called to play a further role, communicating and seeking to influence the wider culture. This happens nowadays primarily through the media. Christian educators' messages should reflect the truth of who they are, what they believe, and how Christian education benefits society. Christian education needs to be seen as for the public good, not merely for its own good. Where possible on issues where Christian educators can agree with the government (or with those who may normally oppose Christian education), Christian educators should seek to work collaboratively. The positive message that education can be a good for all, and that education lifts people out of their current situations, is generally one that Christian educators can endorse and support.

In Western cultures, where the popular narratives are increasingly disconnected with biblical truth, the prevailing trend will be for courts and legislators to follow that trend and make decisions and law antithetical to the operations of Christian schools. The pervasive influence of Western culture globally suggests that other nations should take heed of this trend and prepare themselves for what is likely to come. While Christian educators live in challenging times, they also need to be conscious that in dealings with those in the courts and legislators, the ultimate aim is that they, like the Colossians, "may know the mystery of God, namely, Christ, in whom are hidden all the treasures of wisdom and knowledge" (Colossians 2:2b–3).

Discussion Questions

1. Would you characterize the approach of your Christian school or institution as "protectionist" or "missional"? How might the chosen approach influence the school's future direction?

2. How equipped is your Christian school or institution to deal with the current narratives of popular culture?

3. How aligned are the policies and procedures in your Christian school or institution with your doctrines, tenets, and beliefs?

4. In what ways can your Christian school or institution work collaboratively with others to address these challenges?

Religious Liberties and a Faithful Christian Presence:
Responding to Legal and Legislative Issues in Christian Education

65

Suggested Resources: Religious Freedom and Christians in the Public Discourse

Organizations/Websites

Alliance Defending Freedom (https://www.adflegal.org) is a public policy network of attorneys with a mission to defend religious freedom through offices in Asia, Latin America, Europe, and the U.S. They also provide resources on the defense of religious freedom including formal training programs. *Protecting Your Ministry* is a handbook from Alliance Defending Freedom that covers aspects of operational concerns Christian ministries should consider in the U.S. legal context (**https://www.adflegal.org/campaigns/pym**).

ACSI Legal Legislative Services (https://www.acsi.org/legal-legislative-and-advocacy) identifies and analyzes a broad array of national, legal, and legislative issues. Their work includes tracking legislation and generating reports for all 50 states. With team members both at ACSI Headquarters in Colorado and in Washington, D.C., the team also produces *Legal Legislative Update* three times per year.

Human Rights Law Alliance (https://hrla.org.au/) is an Australian network of lawyers providing support within Australia, similar to ADF.

American Center for Law and Justice (www.aclj.org) was founded in 1990 with the mandate to protect religious and constitutional freedoms. ACLJ engages legal, legislative, and cultural issues by implementing an effective strategy of advocacy, education, and litigation that includes representing clients before the Supreme Court of the United States and international tribunals around the globe.

Publications/Books

The United Nations Universal Declaration of Human Rights (**http://www.un.org/en/universal-declaration-human-rights/**) was first adopted in 1948 and includes several articles that claim religious freedom as a fundamental human right. To date 192 nations have signed the Declaration. These rights are amplified in the International Covenant on Civil and Political Rights (**http://www.ohchr.org/EN/ProfessionalInterest/Pages/CCPR.aspx**) and the Declaration on the Elimination of All Forms of Intolerance and of Discrimination Based on Religion or Belief (**http://www.un.org/documents/ga/res/36/a36r055.htm**).

Free to Serve: Protecting the Religious Freedom of Faith-Based Organizations, by Stephen V. Monsma and Stanley W. Carlson-Thies, Brazos Press, 2015.

Fool's Talk: Recovering the Art of Christian Persuasion, by Os Guinness, InterVarsity Press, 2015.

Uncommon Decency: Christian Civility in an Uncivil World, by Richard J. Mouw, InterVarsity Press Books, 2010.

Suggested Resources: Understanding Contemporary Debates on Gender and Sexuality

Note: The authors provide these resources as reference points to the reader and not necessarily as the singular truth on the topics of human sexuality and the interaction of civil government and religion. The authors do offer them as relevant attempts to engage (mostly) Christian communities in such discussions. The great variation of faithful Christian communities will have varying views as it relates to implications of a faithful presence in society, and consequently the reader is encouraged to engage actively with these resources and not to take them at face value nor simply dismiss them out of hand.

Organizations/Websites

The Center for Faith, Sexuality & Gender. Their mission is to help Christian leaders, churches, and organizations to engage questions about faith, sexuality, and gender with theological depth and pastoral compassion.

American College of Pediatricians (https://www.acpeds.org/the-college-speaks/position-statements/sexuality-issues/gender-identity-issues-in-children-and-adolescents) provides an alternative professional perspective on gender matters.

American Psychological Association LGBT Resources and Publications (**https://www.apa.org/pi/lgbt/resources/**) is one of the most influential voices globally on these issues.

Walt Heyer Ministries (http://waltheyer.com/). Walt Heyer is a former transgendered person with a particular perspective and insight.

Publications/Books

People to Be Loved: Why Homosexuality Is Not Just an Issue, by Preston Sprinkle, Zondervan, 2015.

Washed and Waiting: Reflections on Christian Faithfulness and Homosexuality, by Wesley Hill, Zondervan, 2010.

Secret Thoughts of an Unlikely Convert: An English Professor's Journey into Christian Faith, by Rosaria Champagne Butterfield, Crown & Covenant, 2012.

Openness Unhindered: Further Thoughts of an Unlikely Convert on Sexual Identity and Union with Christ, by Rosaria Champagne Butterfield, Crown & Covenant, 2015.

Giving a Voice to the Voiceless: A Qualitative Study of Reducing Marginalization of Lesbian, Gay, Bisexual and Same-Sex Attracted Students at Christian Colleges and Universities, by Christopher Yuan, Wipf and Stock, 2016.

Religious Liberties and a Faithful Christian Presence:
Responding to Legal and Legislative Issues in Christian Education

67

Understanding Gender Dysphoria: Navigating Transgender Issues in a Changing Culture, by Mark A. Yarhouse, InterVarsity Press, 2015.

"BOYS GIRLS OTHER": Making Sense of the Confusing New World of Gender Identity (**https://www.familyfirst.org.nz/research/gender-2015/**), by Glenn T. Stanton, Research Report commissioned by Family First (New Zealand), 2015.

NOTES

1 American Psychological Association, "Guidelines for Psychological Practice with Transgender and Gender Nonconforming People," *American Psychologist*, 70:9 (2015), 832–864.

Contributors

Dr. Beth Ackerman's passion for children with varying abilities is evident in her professional career as a teacher and principal at a school for children with special needs. She is licensed in elementary education, special education, and administration and supervision. She currently teaches special education courses at Liberty University.

Dhugie Adams worked as a fire fighter and EMT after high school. His desire for authentic, meaningful discipleship brought him to Axis in 2014, where he traveled around North America speaking to students, teachers, and parents. Dhugie now lives full-time in Colorado Springs, working as the Director of Growth and Impact at Axis.

Gavin Brettenny, BA, BEd, MOL, has 20 years of Christian school leadership as principal of a Christian high school and director of a K–12 South African Christian school. He currently serves as the ACSI Director of Strategic Development, Africa and on the directors' team of Black Forest Academy, an international Christian school in Germany.

Dr. William E. Brown led two Christian universities as president. He has written several books and more than 100 articles for journals, magazines, and encyclopedias. As the Senior Fellow for Worldview and Culture at the Chuck Colson Center for Christian Worldview, he directs the Colson Fellows Program, an international fellowship program.

Paul Campey is a partner with Resolve Consulting Group based in Australia, working all across the world helping schools and other Christian organizations with their governance, strategic planning, and financial management. He holds an MBA and is a chartered accountant, and has been in and around Christian schools for over 22 years.

Dr. James L. Drexler is Dean of Education at Covenant College, Lookout Mountain, Georgia. After a 23-year career in middle and secondary education, Drexler moved to Covenant in 2004. Among his publications are *Schools as Communities* (Purposeful Design Publications 2007) and *Nurturing the School Community* (Purposeful Design Publications 2011).

Dr. Dan Egeler, President of ACSI, is passionate about teaching communication as an art. A storyteller and the author of *Mentoring Millennials: Shaping the Next Generation*, Dan has also been a teacher, coach, and principal.

Dr. Gene Frost earned his undergraduate degree from Wheaton College, his MDiv from Northern Seminary, and his EdD from Northern Illinois University. Gene has served as a pastor, teacher, business executive, board member, and currently as the head of school at Wheaton Academy. He is the author of *Learning from the Best, Volumes One and Two* (Purposeful Design Publications 2007).

Joel R. Gaines serves as the assistant head of the upper school at Delaware County Christian School. He is married to Tia and has one son, Josiah, and three daughters, Hosanna, Elaina, and Adoniah. He graduated from Philadelphia Biblical University (Cairn University) with a BS in Education and Biblical Studies, and earned an MEd in Education from Cabrini University. Joel has served in multiple roles over the past ten years in both Christian and public education, in both urban and suburban settings.

Dr. Connie Z. Mitchell is the Dean of the College of Education at Columbia International University, where she has served on the faculty since 1991. She desires to support educators in their quest to serve as teachers and educational leaders, sustained with a Christian philosophy of education and a global vision.

Dr. Barrett Mosbacker is head of school for Westminster Christian Academy, Saint Louis, Missouri. He is also an adjunct professor at Covenant College teaching school business management in the graduate program. Prior to his work in Christian education, Dr. Mosbacker worked for several U.S. corporations and as a management consultant to the Legal Services Corp., Washington, D.C. He received his doctorate in educational leadership from the University of North Carolina, Charlotte.

Brian Mueller has served as president of Grand Canyon University since 2008, guiding the remarkable transformation of a financially troubled university into a nearly $3 billion institution that has become a driving force in higher education today. Mr. Mueller, who earned an MEd and a BA in education from Concordia University, also spent 22 years at the Apollo Group where he served as president and grew the University of Phoenix online platform from 3,000 students to 240,000 in an eight-year time frame.

Dr. Stephen G. Reel has served for 27 years in Christian school ministry as a Bible teacher, school administrator, and adjunct professor. He serves at ACSI as the Vice President, USA and is the author of *Clear Focus: Rediscovering the Most Important Aspect of Christian School Ministry* (2015). He and his wife, Melanie, have three children.

Dr. Glen Schultz is the director of Kingdom Education Ministries. He has been involved in education for the past 49 years and is the author of *Kingdom Education* (LifeWay Press 1998). He received his BA degree from Roberts Wesleyan College and his MEd and EdD from the University of Virginia.

Philip Scott's background is a blend of education, religion, and law. He has taught middle and high school students in Christian schools. He is twice a graduate of Liberty University in education and from their law school, and has studied theology and law at the Southern Baptist Theological Seminary. He currently serves as ACSI's in-house counsel.

Mark Spencer, FCA, GAICD, B. Bus, M. Lab. Rel. & Law, Grad. Dip. Legal Studies, is the Executive Officer, National Policy for Christian Schools Australia. He commenced serving Christian schools in 1990. Mark has held a variety of board and political roles. He is married to Melanie, a Christian school leader, with three children.

Janet Stump is Director of Development for The Colossian Forum, Grand Rapids, Michigan. For fourteen years Jan served in leadership at ACSI as Executive Director of the ACSI Education Foundation and as Director of Development and Public Relations. She has a master's degree in literature from the University of Alaska Anchorage and is a certified fund raising executive (CFRE).

Dr. Lynn E. Swaner is the Director of Thought Leadership and Higher Education Initiatives at ACSI. Prior to ACSI, she served as a Christian school administrator and a graduate professor of education. A published scholar, her focus is on engaged pedagogy and creating cultures that foster student learning. She received her EdD from Teachers College, Columbia University, in New York City.